D0323514

ON TEAMS

Ron Archer

with
Janet Bond Wood

ON TEAMS

IRWIN
Professional Publishing®
Chicago • London • Singapore

Times Mirror
Higher Education Group

Library of Congress Cataloging-in-Publication Data

Archer, Ron J., (date)
   On teams / Ron Archer with Janet Bond Wood.
      p. cm.
   Includes index.
   ISBN 0–7863–0498–7
   1. Work groups. 2. Employee empowerment. 3. Work groups—Case studies. I. Wood, Janet Bond. II. Title.
   HD66.A728 1997
   658.4′036—dc20   96–21833

Printed in the United States of America
1 2 3 4 5 6 7 8 9 1 DOC 3 2 1 0 9 8 7 6

ACKNOWLEDGMENTS

Writing a book is a lot like the example of the old turtle sitting on top of a high fence post. You know he didn't get there by himself. He had a lot of help. I feel the same way about *On Teams*. I had significant contributions from many wonderful and committed people who shared the vision of this completed text.

First, my special thanks go to Janet Bond Wood, whose writing skills and literary insight enabled me to put my 15 years of experience as a team-building consultant and an international motivational speaker in book form. She transformed my ideas and thoughts into vivid word pictures and helped me clearly communicate the complexities of organizational development and team maturation.

I am also grateful to the fine professionals at Irwin Professional Publishing for the privilege of working with them to produce my first book. I would like to thank Cynthia Zigmund, Senior Editor at Irwin, who provided me with all the tools and all the support I needed to complete this project. She showed tremendous patience and concern through her continued motivation, coaching, and guidance, especially during the loss of my father. I would also like to thank Rick Riddering who attended a team-building seminar that I conducted in Chicago some years ago and suggested that my experiences and expertise be put in book form.

I remain appreciative to the staff at Executive Center Business Support Services of Cleveland for their assistance in transforming my handwritten notes into readable drafts.

Special thanks to friends, coaches, and players in the NFL with whom I have had the privilege of working—through them I learned a great deal about the challenges of professional team development. My associations with the Cleveland Browns gave me tremendous insight into the world of teamwork at the highest level. I thank Richard Mann, former offensive coach for the Browns, for his friendship and insights on teams. I thank Stephen Braggs, former defensive back for the Cleveland Browns, who was instrumental in putting together our team development training program for corporations and colleges. I thank Ho Davidson, former Bowling Green University Football standout and one-time Miami Dolphin, for his friendship and insights on team development.

I thank my staff, past and present, at the Archer Institute for their hours of research and data collection that went into the development of this book. Special mention goes to Don Krumweide, Guinn Ellis, Patrick O'Neil, Marijo Shuntich, and a very special thanks to April Archer, Cynthia Hughes, and Patricia Archer who held it all together in the early days of this process and never once doubted that we would get to this point in time.

Finally, to my best friend, my helpmate, and my partner in life, my wife Cynthia Archer, who read every line of this book at least 50 times in perfecting the content. I couldn't have done it without you! At last I can officially say it is finished.

To Ashley and Christopher Archer,

May this book serve as an inspiration as you grow and develop into what God has planned for you. Remember always that what seems impossible with man is possible with God.

Love,
Daddy

CONTENTS

THREE

FOUR

FIVE

SIX

Coral Springs, Florida: "We Want To Be the Premier City in Florida to Live, Work, and Raise a Family" 101

Some Background 103
The Change Process 107
The New Government Organization 108
The City Garage—One Motivated Team 110
Quality Is Never Done 115

SEVEN

Team Tools for Development and Delight 119

Activity 1: Just before the Tropical Island Experience 120
Evaluating the Activity 123
Team Decision Making 125
Activity 2: Collaboration Can Be Fun 129
Evaluating the Activity 130
Activity 3: The Blind Leading the Blind 131
Evaluating the Activity 132
Activity 4: Brainstorming for Teams 133
Activity 5: Careful Listening, Better Hearing 135
Evaluating the Activity 136
Activity 6: Talk to People (TTP) 138
Evaluating the Activity 139

INTRODUCTION

Thank you for considering *On Teams* in your quest for further information about a significant movement that is sweeping our culture. If we do nothing else, we would like to convince you of the power of teamwork in your life, your business, your organization, your PTA, or your church. With teams we can approach problems more resourcefully than we ever could working alone. This is absolutely true. In a successful team you have a group of people working toward a shared purpose with a mutuality and respect for one another that breeds success.

We hope you'll find in this book the encouragement you are looking for and the motivation you seek to become a true team player.

Chapter 1 provides general information about the nature of teams. The most important idea you can get from this chapter is that teams aren't a project, they are a process. Teams are as alive as the humans that form them—teams, in fact, are organisms.

Chapter 2 brings up the *e* word. That's right, *empowerment*. You can't have an authentic team without a sense of empowerment among its members. Team members need to know they may do (have permission to do) what they can do (are capable of doing). Without empowerment as a fundamental step you've just got another management flavor-of-the-month that leaves a cynical taste on the tongue.

Chapter 3 is all about the preparation for implementing healthy teams. It's about knowing the difference between incubation and incineration—incubation is what you do to organisms so they can grow; incineration is what you do to germs and toxic waste to destroy them.

Chapter 4 gets into the difficulties of team building, and difficulties abound as they do in any challenging task. After all, learning to think "we" instead of just "me" is really hard.

Chapters 5 and 6 are stories of two organizations' experiences with team building. Hillside Hospital traveled a gravelly road through major labor-management hostilities into the upside-down world of competitive health care in the 1990s. They are successful now with teams. For the city of Coral Springs, moving to teams makes it possible for the city commissioners to run their city more like a business, more efficiently and with better quality service.

Chapter 7 is a selection of some of the training exercises from the Archer Institute's training programs. Through these exercises we work on issues of development, decision making, and communication.

We also have fun, and so, we hope, will you!

ONE

Teams—What They're All About

Alexander the Great, during one of his early campaigns to conquer the world, invaded a small island just off the coast of Greece. When Alexander and his troops landed and surveyed the situation, they looked out across the hilltops and realized that they were outnumbered five to one. His troops, overwhelmed and afraid, began a retreat back to their ships. Alexander, sensing his troops' fear and panic, ordered them to light a bonfire to keep the advancing army at bay. His troops lit the bonfire and watched as it spread rapidly down the beachhead. As Alexander had hoped, the fire spread and ignited their own ships. With their ships afire, Alexander stood on a mound and addressed his troops. His speech was one of the most inspiring, moving, and motivational ever delivered. He simply said to the group, "Now, my friends, either we win or we die."

When a paradigm changes either you are on the way or you are in the way! At this moment in our economic history, American organizations are facing the same challenges that Alexander's troops faced as

> *When a paradigm changes, either you are on the way or you are in the way!*

they watched their ships burn. To put it in modern terms: Either we change our collective mind-sets and organizational structures so we can move forward, or we die.

One of the critical challenges facing American organizations as they approach the new millennium is their past success—the organizational assumption that "what has made us successful up to now will continue to make us successful." This notion prevails in spite of what has been called the Three Cs of the millennium: overwhelming complexity, increasing competition, and accelerated change.

If American institutions and organizations are going to be able to gain and then sustain a global competitive advantage, they must make a philosophical break with the past. The days of dividing the work into the heads and the hands must end. Simplistic notions of blue and white collars, labor and professional, union and nonunion are impediments that must be burned because they are tools of the past and, to the extent that we refuse to put them down, burdens for the future.

> *If American institutions and organizations are going to be able to gain and then sustain a global competitive advantage, they must make a philosophical break with the past.*

The answer as shown in Figure 1–1 sounds simple: flatten those hierarchical structures so that your organization can respond more quickly to its lifeblood, the customer! Replace old notions of top-down command with the philosophy of leadership and empowerment so that your employees can communicate with the customer with some responsibility and integrity. Build an organization that is lean, lithe, and flexible so it can move quickly and respond to, or even anticipate, opportunities. What will this new organization be like? It's a team! Teams can

Figure 1–1 The Modern Look   Organizations are trying to move from Company A's structure to Company B's structure when they move toward teamwork. Company B is much closer to the customer and thus better able to know what the customer wants.

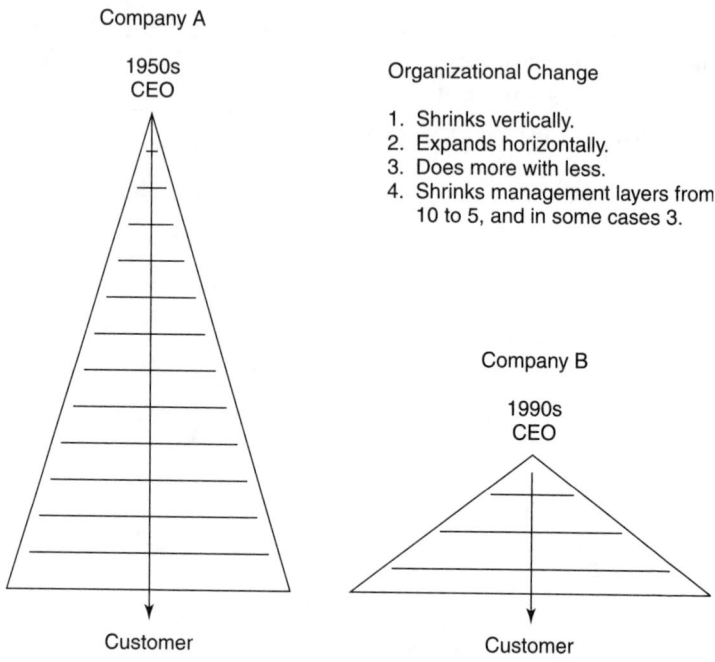

Company A

1950s
CEO

Organizational Change

1. Shrinks vertically.
2. Expands horizontally.
3. Does more with less.
4. Shrinks management layers from 10 to 5, and in some cases 3.

Company B

1990s
CEO

Customer

Customer

be built to accomplish any task. They can be project oriented, self-directed, or cross-functional. Their membership can change—a team can be successful and then disband only to reform for a new project, challenge, or goal.

To implement teams successfully, an organization must create the proper culture in which these teams can survive and thrive. A team is more of an organism than it is an organization, and implementing teams in an organization is more of a process than a project. As an organism, a team has a life cycle. Its growth can be plotted through distinct stages of development. What does a team need to help it grow through its various stages of development successfully? More than anything else a team needs an organizational culture that allows it to be a self-directing organism.

A team is more of an organism than it is an organization, and implementing teams in an organization is more of a process than a project.

In 15 years of professional team building and organizational coaching, I have learned that some organizations have a mind-set and a culture that is diametrically opposed to the entire self-directed team concept. I have seen that many managers attempt to transform their organizations with empowerment and quality initiatives while they hold on to past paradigms that almost guarantee the initiatives' failure. They are so blinded by their past glories they do not realize that many of these antiquated policies, practices, mind-sets, and structures are strangling their future success.

If You Want Healthy Fish . . .

Let's say you have a pond that is full of fish all trying to maximize their potential. The fish, however, are not doing so well; in fact, they are very ill. They are ill because the pond in which they live and work is contaminated, dirty, and toxic. Over the years it has been used as a dumping ground for benzene, trichloroethylene, and Freon™. The owner of the pond recognizes the fish are not well and calls in an expert to solve the problem. The owner tells the consultant to fix the fish. The consultant takes the fish out of the dirty pond water and puts them temporarily in a clean holding tank full of fresh sparkling mineral water. The fish are fed well, exercised, and after 60 days, they are revitalized and reenergized. They have recovered! The owner takes the fish and puts them back into the same dirty pond water. The fish don't remain healthy for too long in spite of all the money and effort spent on trying to make them better because nothing is done to change the condition of the pond water.

To change the pond water is to change the surrounding culture, the mind-set, the policies, the practices of the past. Why are so many organizations unwilling to change the pond water, the culture, in which their teams are asked to thrive? And why, then, do managers wonder at the failure that occurs so often? How many organizations do you know that have managers who are confusing activity with accomplishment, managers who are so busy setting up quality circles, talk-back groups, and other activities that they don't see the whole picture: those fish won't ever be able to function until the water is cleaned up!

Companies have reengineered and have identified the issues, practices, and policies that stifle innovation, smother creativity, and hamper productivity. Organizations have downsized and rightsized (or as they say in southern California, "We are going to bring you in and free up your future!"). But through all this activity, very little has been accomplished. Why? What is holding us back?

Once upon A Paradigm

There once was a bold, brave paradigm pioneer who loved to walk the high wire across national wonders. He had dared to do the impossible by successfully walking on a high wire across the Grand Canyon in Arizona. He also had walked across an active volcano in Hawaii. He was applauded and revered for his courage and daring. Yet in spite of all his accomplishments there was still one natural wonder he had not challenged, Niagara Falls. He decided that he would walk across the Falls from the Canadian side to the American side. He announced his vision to the world. He had a kickoff celebration with media representatives present. The date and the time were set.

The day of the walk, large crowds gathered at both sides of the Falls. He started his daring jaunt to the unknown. He walked directly over the midpoint of the Falls and with the water churning below, he stopped for a moment to focus on the task remaining. He finally arrived on the American side where he stood on a high platform and began talking to the enormous crowd that had gathered below. He shouted out to the crowd below, "How many believe I can walk backwards across the Falls?" The crowd began to chant back, "We believe, we believe, we believe!" He yelled back to the crowd again, "How many believe I can walk backwards across the Falls blindfolded without using my balance beam?" and the crowd, now in a frenzy, screamed back, "We believe, we believe, we believe!" He then called to the crowd, "Who then will go with me?" and suddenly a hushed silence fell over the crowd at the bank of the Falls. Humiliated by their lack of belief, they dispersed.

I have been invited to address conventions filled with high-power professionals from varying backgrounds and interests, and I have listened as these professionals boldly yell out in board rooms and convention halls the unified crescendo of, "We believe in self-directed work teams. We believe in employee empowerment. We believe in a customer-focused organization. We believe in the value of team compensation." Then when I ask, "How many of you are willing to take the necessary steps to significantly transform your organizational cultures, archaic compensation systems, and turn-of-the-century management structures?" a hushed silence falls over many board rooms, counsel chambers, and union halls across the country.

I have discovered that many American organizations want to use their old models to create a new structure, and it just does not work. The unwillingness of top management to truly empower their workforce and the unwillingness of unions to rethink competency over seniority is causing more than a few groups to confuse activity with accomplishment. At the risk of being trite, this stuck-ness amounts to a fear of real change, the kind of change that paradigm shifts and burning boats is all about. We must change employee mind-sets and organizational structures simultaneously for lasting positive change to occur.

> *I have discovered that many American organizations want to use their old models to create a new structure, and it just does not work.*

Starting in the Same Sandbox

We need to understand two things to progress together through this book: teams and history. We need to have the same understanding about where all this emphasis on teams is coming from, or at least we all need to understand where *I* say this is all coming from.

Did you ever stop to ask the question, "Who said that the top-down hierarchical management structure was the most effective means of managing people and producing goods?" With all the talk about the information highway, super-computer chips, virtual realities, and space shuttles and colonies, the management systems still in use in government, in many of our most beloved institutions, and in our corporations are modeled after a turn-of-the-century hundred-year-old philosophy developed by Frederick Winslow Taylor, the grandfather of scientific management. The philosophy

With all the talk about the information highway, super-computer chips, virtual realities, and space shuttles and colonies, the management systems still in use in government, in many of our most beloved institutions, and in our corporations are modeled after a turn-of-the-century hundred-year-old philosophy developed by Frederick Winslow Taylor, the grandfather of scientific management.

of Frederick Taylor influenced the thinking of giants like Henry Ford, John Rockefeller, and many other early 20th-century industrialists. Figure 1–2 captures what Taylor's scientific model looked like and often sounded like.

Frederick Taylor taught and firmly believed that the most efficient and effective way to run an organization was to divide the workers into the heads and the hands, the thinkers and the doers, and may the two never meet. He thought the best way to produce quality goods was to command and control the masses in tightly supervised shops. He also taught that the best way to manage a largely unskilled and poorly educated workforce was to break down job responsibilities into small specialized increments. The workers would become proficient more rapidly, and a sense of order and control could be imposed on the emerging chaos of industrialization. Uniformity and conformity were valued over creativity and innovation. The worker was viewed as an extension of the machines he or she operated. The scientific management organizational model worked extremely well up until about 1973, when the rest of the world began to catch up with us.

Japan, particularly, had embraced W. Edwards Deming, a man whose lessons on quality were rapidly

> *Frederick Taylor taught and firmly believed that the most efficient and effective way to run an organization was to divide the workers into the heads and the hands, the thinkers and the doers, and may the two never meet.*

Figure 1–2 Fredick Winslow Taylor's Scientific Management Model

Unfortunately, even today many companies still practice Mr. Taylor's method of management.

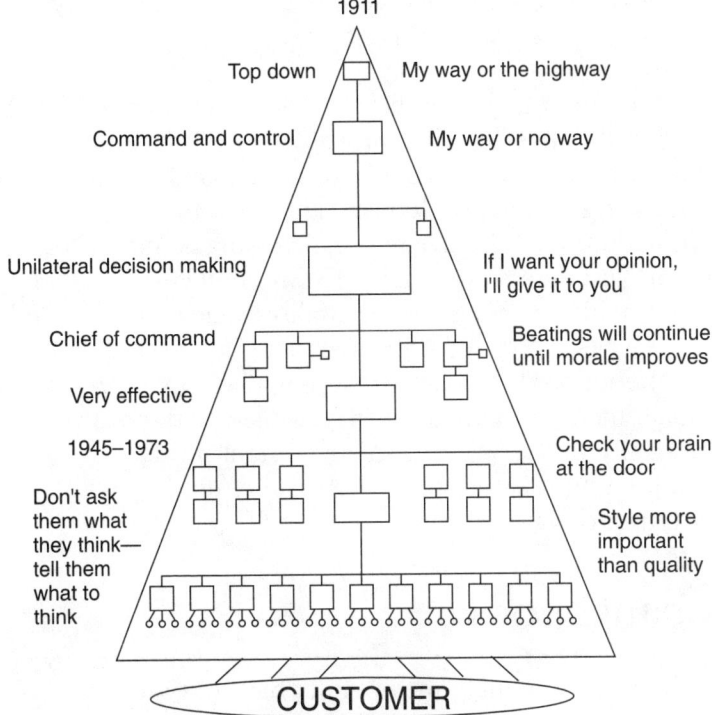

changing the American consumer's notion that Asian goods mean "cheap" to the idea that Japanese goods mean "quality." In Japan, because of the destruction of the war, companies were working with an almost clean sheet of paper. They were able to adopt much of Deming's quality theories and implement the ideas with a process geared to accomplishment. In Japan, workers and managers walked the talk. The companies that emerged in the 1950s and 1960s were flatter than their fatter competitors in America. With our scientific management model, worker's hands were tied because the workers were overmanaged. American corporations were spending lots of time and money on layers of middle management that were not directly tied to product development, implementation, or innovation.

More than 20 years ago, American companies began getting the message that all was not well. Heeding what we heard, we've made some accomplishments improving quality, cycle time, and customer service. We have broached programmatic changes and called them paradigm shifts, things like reengineering, TQM (total quality management), quality circles, empowered employees, and teams. But we have not been able to get the leopard to change its spots. Our managers today, most of them, are still schooled in the old war mentality of the scientific management model. We are still fighting the culture change and struggling with dirty pond water.

Change, or Die

Our need to change, meanwhile, has continued to grow. The demographics of the American workforce are radically different from what they were in 1945. In *Workforce 2000,* the U.S. Department of Labor and the Hudson Institute report that by the year 2003, 85 percent of the new entry-level workers will be made up of women who leave the home to join the workplace and of people of color—African Americans, Asian Americans, Hispanic Americans. These new workers bring significant cultural attachments, some ethnically based, some generationally based, to the workplace as independent thinkers who do not automatically respond with respect to authority figures.

The reasons to burn ships are growing by the moment.

It Is Too How You Play

Now, what do we mean by *teams?* Many of you have had an experience being on a team. In school you may have been on a sports team, but you may not have considered the staff of the yearbook or the newspaper, or the members of your high school chorus, to be a team. In fact, any group of people brought together for a common purpose is a team when each member of that group is recognized as an equal partner with the others.

In the workplace, there are many different kinds of teams: self-directed, cross-functional, project, pilot, ad-hoc, and quality. Some teams come together for one project of a week's duration, and some teams work together for a year or longer. Teams in a company may share members with each other, yet each team might have a different goal. Who sets the goals, how team members buy into them, who builds the teams, and how they are managed for progress and quality measurement are all significant questions. These questions also can represent significant problems for

> *In fact, any group of people brought together for a common purpose is a team when each member of that group is recognized as an equal partner with the others.*

teams in different stages of development. In the next chapters we'll talk about the different kinds of teams and the problems they face.

Today, wherever quality is a buzzword, the notion of teams is sure to follow. It's as important to understand how to be an employee and a team member, an organism within an organization, as it is to understand how to help your organization manage change in its attempts to manage the agents of change—Hey, that's you, the team!

TWO

What Exactly Is an Empowered Team?

When I think about successful teams today, many images come to mind: the mighty Green Bay Packers team of the 1960s that won five championships within seven years and three consecutive world championships. I think of the U.S. Olympic Hockey Team that shocked the world and beat the more experienced and more talented Russian team at Lake Placid, New York, in the 1980 Winter Olympic Games. I also think about GM's Saturn Project Team, which proved that American companies could compete with the Japanese and build a high-quality, affordable small car.

What is it about some groups that enables them to overcome great odds and difficulties to form a cohesive unit while other groups flounder and lack the cohesion and synergy to be a successful team?

In this chapter we are going to define *empowered teams* and look at the 10 characteristics that separate successful winning teams from those that confuse activity with accomplishment. We will also look at the benefits and the barriers of developing teams and organizations today.

A Working Organism

An empowered team is a dynamic group of individuals who have the skills, the training, and the authority to manage themselves and the work they do with the guidance and the motivation of a coach. Although not a member of the team, it is the coach's responsibility to see that the team succeeds. Every team also has a leader, chosen from and eventually by, its members. The leader will, when necessary, make the unilateral decisions that are called for in a crisis. The leader will also keep track of the team's goals, problems, and schedules. Teams enjoy the privileges and accept the responsibility of empowerment as well as the challenges of continuous improvement. Teams range in size, optimally, from 5 to 15. They are organized around a common objective and are responsible for a final product or a whole work process that is delivered to an internal or external user or customer.

An empowered team is a cohesive unit of highly motivated, highly skilled, and properly trained people who supervise themselves with the encouragement and direction of a coach.

The reason that I suggest a team size of 5 to 15 is simply this: In my work with teams, I have found teams that are larger than 15 to be too cumbersome, too large to be able to nimbly reach the synergistic, cohesive consensus for making team decisions—too many minds, too many personalities, too much distraction. If your team is smaller than five, you have the danger of developing what is called *group think.* That's where one strong personality can influence, sway, or intimidate others to his or her point of view. If this happens, you lose the possibility of achieving the potential that led to team building in the first place.

What Is Empowerment?

Few words in American organizations today polarize people as effectively as the word *empowerment*. For some, empowerment is nothing short of a front-line worker coup d'etat, a recipe for anarchy-in-a-moment, and for others it is nothing more than the management flavor of the month, buzzword of the day, fake it until you make it.

The reaction to the idea of empowerment is almost like a parent whose child swallowed four marbles, and the parent runs to the emergency room, grabs the attending physician, and says, "Doctor, my child is going to die! He swallowed four marbles. Do something." The doctor, very calm and relaxed, says to the parent, "Just have a seat. It is going to be okay." The parent says, exasperated, "What do you mean it's going to be okay! The kid has swallowed four marbles!" The doctor says, "Just watch and wait and you will see. This too shall pass." That's how many employees (and, more cynically, quite a few managers) today view this thing we call empowerment.

Let's start by saying what empowerment is *not*. "Empowerment Programs" are schemes and ideas that an elite group of executives generates, incubates, and hatches. These executives communicate in a formal directive that from now until the end of time we/you are going to work in this new way until further notice—NOT. That kind of empowerment program is an oxymoron like "jumbo shrimp" or "icy hot." The managers and employees who are directed to be empowered this way never understand clearly why it is being done, what it really means to them and their jobs, and when this whole thing is really supposed to happen. Many organizations try to sell this new bottom-up employee-involved concept while still using the old top-down managerial style, and the two just do not fit. It's back to trying to fix the fish without changing the pond water.

So what, then, is empowerment? Empowerment is an attitude that reflects a belief that the people who do the work every day have the knowledge, the insight, and the experience to plan, implement, and control the work processes as well as the ability to accept responsibility for quality, costs, and scheduling. To empower requires of the people in positions of power a readiness and willingness to evaluate their controls and transfer power and authority for significant areas of judgment and decision making to the people performing specific tasks. It also requires more of the people being empowered—they will have to work harder, but it will probably be more fun.

The major barrier that prevents empowerment from taking hold is trust, or the lack thereof. Employees mistrust management motives, and managers mistrust employee willingness to fully participate and take advantage of the opportunities empowerment provides. Managers, who also feel

> *Empowerment is an attitude that reflects a belief that the people who do the work every day have the knowledge, the insight, and the experience to plan, implement, and control the work processes as well as the ability to accept responsibility for quality, costs, and scheduling.*

threatened by the uncertainty of the initiative, find themselves reacting against empowerment and for self-preservation. True empowerment requires four things:

1. A team has the authority to make the decisions necessary to accomplish its task.
2. The team has some input in setting the task or goal(s).
3. The team receives the appropriate resources, training, and coaching to be successful.
4. The team is held responsible and accountable for reaching its preset goals and objectives.

Each of these four cornerstones—authority, input, resources/training, and accountability—is critical to a successful empowerment initiative, so I want to take some time to look at each of these elements more closely.

Authority

Why is it difficult for some managers today to transfer real power and real authority to a front-line team? One of the major reasons is the training in management science–culture our managers received. We have trained our managers and supervisors how to act in a top-down, authoritative environment for the past 100 years. Today managers feel that they are getting mixed messages from the organizations in which they work. On the one hand, the manager's superiors say, "Empower your people. Let go of authority. Create kumbaya." But in the fine print of that glorious message is the warning, "Oh, and by the way, if this empowerment thing does not work, we are coming after you. Good luck."

If the New York Jets, for example, lose 12 games this year, the owners are not going to fire the New York Jets. They are going to come after the coach, and he knows this. So in the midst of all the pomp and circumstance about letting go of authority and trusting your employees, remember that if it results in failure, the team may survive but the manager may not. This lesson, by the way, has significant import for the way the team is selected. One of the things a new coach for the New York Jets is going to do, after all, is either kick butt or get a new quarterback as he did with Neil O'Donnell.

While managers grapple with mixed messages about empowerment, team members also are frustrated when they see the promise of more authority, input, resources, and accountability turn out to be nothing more than a hallucination generated by the heat of transformation. These are the true reflections, though, of problems with the pond water.

It is a very difficult time to be a manager in the midst of this paradigm shift. Many times managers find themselves the bridge between two very different worlds, between two very different generations and two very different mind-sets. One is the command-and-control model. The other is dynamic, progressive, and independent and demands more authority. So how do managers trained in the command-and-control model meet the expectations set by their superiors, who are still operating out of the command-and-control model, and yet create a culture where empowered teams can survive and thrive?

First, change takes time, understanding, and mutual respect for what is being attempted. If everyone has bought into the new order, then when the going gets tough that agreement can serve as a touchstone. This is risky, because everyone is vulnerable as he or she learns the new skills. True change is very scary. Empowered teams must develop empathy and understanding for the problems today's managers face.

> *Change takes time, understanding, and mutual respect for what is being attempted.*

If managers could have a sense of humor about the situation they would see that the organization's process is the same as the psychological trauma that a parent goes through with a child who has just turned 16 years old and can now legally drive the family car. Now, how many parents actually say, "Well, you've turned 16, that's great! Here are the keys to the family car. Oh, by the way here is the gas credit card, fill it up, go, drive, have fun, have a great day. I trust you, and I'll see you sometime this evening." I don't think so. Most parents that I know will say, "Oh, you're 16 now. That's nice. Here are the keys to the family car. Just sniff them. You want to drive this car that is in my name by yourself in this city? Not today. Oh, no. If you want to drive this car, I will be riding with you. You want to go to the mall, I will be there; pick up your friends, I'll be there; go visit, I'll be there." The kid is allowed to start the car in the driveway, maybe back the car out of the driveway, possibly park the car next to the curb on the street.

The Three Cs for Developing Trust

So how does real empowerment occur? Before empowerment can really happen the conduit of trust has to be established through which authority and power will be transferred. So how is trust established? Psychologically, the manager has to be able to see what I call the three Cs:

Before empowerment can really happen the conduit of trust has to be established through which authority and power will be transferred.

1. **Competence.** The employees have passed a series of tests, met training requirements, and shown an understanding of the complexity and the responsibility of their tasks. They can demonstrate they know what they are doing. They understand and can do what is required of them.

2. **Confidence.** The manager has to have some assurance that the employees can make decisions, especially under pressure.

3. **Consistency.** The manager has to know that employees can demonstrate the above characteristics effectively over a specific period of time. The employees need to become unconsciously competent—able to act appropriately when there is no time to think about it.

When a manager is able to see the three Cs with great clarity over an extended period of time (12 to 18 months), trust is established that the team can meet the challenges ahead—they have what it takes. Don't forget, though, that developing trust requires significant effort from everyone.

I would say that 80 percent of today's managers truly want to empower their teams, but are struggling with how to do it so it makes sense to them and to their teams. They want to know how to help their teams mature and develop. You see, if we think back to our fledgling and the understandably anxious parents, one reason the parent lets go of the car keys is the realization that being a chauffeur is confining, draining, and inconvenient—always having to take this kid to the mall, or the ballgame, or soccer practice, or a friend's house is a burden. The practice has ceased to be effective.

Managers are facing overwhelming complexity as the span of control increases from 1 to 7 employees, to 1 to 20, to 1 to 60. They are being asked to do more with less. Managers will also discover that trying to chauffeur their groups through every decision-making process is simply too straining, not practical, and not efficient. It no longer works. We'll talk more about management's special involvement in building teams that work in Chapter 4.

> *Managers will also discover that trying to chauffeur their groups through every decision-making process is simply too straining, not practical, and not efficient. It no longer works.*

Input

After authority has been transferred you need to help your people learn how to use their power. Empowerment is not doing something to people as much as it is doing something with people. In order to create a cohesive culture in which teams will survive, thrive, and mature, team members, your people, must have a voice in the issues that will affect them directly.

For you managers, I want to stress the difference between casually being involved with something and being personally committed to something. You see, casual involvement and personal commitment is very similar to ham and eggs. With ham and eggs the chicken was casually involved; the pig was personally committed. One could lay and walk away, and one was there to stay. Managers, you need to be personally committed to the success of this venture in order for it to succeed.

Once you have clearly communicated to the team the problem or goal that brought it into being, you can help the team develop its own mission and vision statements. After establishing task parameters, or whatever appropriate parameters are necessary for the team to understand its purpose—why it exists—you can ask its members what they think about issues and problems and how they will resolve certain complaints. Also on your list of things to do for success is to lead the team through a needs assessment and have a direct hand in developing the team training curriculum.

Remember, people tend to honor, support, respect, and even defend, what they help to create. Is it your idea, coach, or is it our idea? As the German philosopher Hegel once wrote, "Truth is not found in a thesis nor is truth found in the antithesis, but truth is found in the emergent synthesis that reconciles those two extremes."

> *Remember, people tend to honor, support, respect, and even defend, what they help to create.*

By allowing people on your team to collaborate on decision making, you generate in them a sense of ownership of the problem and the solution, and ownership in turn creates a sense of empowerment. Dr. Martin Luther King once wrote these profound words, "There is nothing more dangerous than for a group to feel as though they have no stake in a nation, organization, or community; for then the group feels that by destroying it, they have nothing to lose."

During this process, you will not only be giving input to your team, you will be getting input from them. How do you get this to happen? You may have to employ the Socratic method, ask some probing questions: "How would you resolve this issue? Why is this customer important to us? What training topics are important to this group?" Remember, people make decisions to change for their reasons not your reasons. When you allow people to have input on a decision, a plan of action, you are saying to them that they are important. They are an important part of the

> *Remember, people make decisions to change for their reasons not your reasons.*

process. Whoever we listen to, we value. Whoever we do not listen to, we devalue. Allow people to have input on decisions affecting their team and their work. Make certain, too, that you stay involved. You have input in their success; the team has input in where it needs to go to accomplish its goals.

Resources

The third cornerstone for creating an empowered team and a healthy, sustaining environment in which a team can thrive is provisions. In this case we're talking about providing the necessary and appropriate resources. By resources we mean the money for training, the tools for work, and the access to those tools. By providing resources, you show the team that the organization is serious, even committed to their success. As we said in the first chapter, a team is more like an organism than it is like an organization. It follows, then, that team building is more of a process than a single project. As an organism, your team will grow if your organization provides the following:

1. Interpersonal skills training.
2. Cross-training technical skills.
3. Administrative skills training.
4. Team compensation/reward systems that support developing proficiency in the above.

1. INTERPERSONAL SKILLS TRAINING

During the early stages of team development, the first 9 to 12 months, 80 percent of your major problems are going to be interpersonal in nature and not technical. For this reason I recommend that you refresh your knowledge of the four Cs of interpersonal skills.

The Four Cs Revisit *communication* skills. Remember that only 38 percent of communication is transferred by the tone of your voice, 55 percent of communication is transferred by your nonverbal body language, and only 7 percent of interpersonal communication is transferred by your words, jargon, or pedantic nomenclature. That adds up to mean that 93 percent of interpersonal communication is nonverbal, attached directly to the person. It is called the medium; it *is* the message.

The next C is *conflict resolution*. Provide your team members with training that helps them understand how to give constructive criticism, how to give constructive feedback, how to disagree without being disagreeable, and that tact is having the ability to make a point without making an enemy. Team members need to learn how to focus their feedback on the issue, not on the person.

The third C is *consensus building*. One of the most effective ways for an empowered team to reach some decisions is by consensus. Now, consensus does not mean total group agreement. It means that we agree enough as a team to be able to fully support the team's final decision. It means that you may have 75 percent buy-in by all the individuals. It means that I may not love this decision, but I can live with it.

The fourth C is *coaching*. Team members need to learn how to coach one another when a team is struggling. Encouragement and discipline are also important coaching skills. Managers especially need to know how to be able to constructively coach a team through the difficulties of team transformation.

2. Cross-Training Technical Skills

Cross-training technical skills is important to develop professional empathy and intimacy on the team. Cross-training creates a flexible attitude among team members. It is like a baseball game. You have a center fielder, you have a left fielder, you have a right fielder. A fly ball is hit out to center field. The right fielder dashes over and steps in front of the center fielder and makes the catch for the third out. Are they upset with one another? As long as the team wins, people can be very flexible about being cross-trained. The attitudes of "that's not my job," "that's not my problem," and "that's not my fault" can evaporate with effective cross-training.

In cases where cross-training would be an unrealistic expectation, for example, a surgical team in which members possess distinct expertise that results from specialized intensive training, I recommend what is called *cross-pollination*. Cross-pollination requires learning enough information about each job to gain the following:

- A common language with which to accurately communicate and solve problems.
- Objectives and goals that are mutually understood and agreed upon.
- Enhanced perception to assist one another intelligently and to be able to ask intelligent questions to resolve problems.

3. Administrative Skills Training

The third provision for team success is administrative skills training. It deals with the management of the team's time, budget, resources, and space. Training must be offered in the topics of time management, conducting team performance appraisals, running efficient team meetings, and budget allocation. Without administrative skills training, the team will confuse activity with accomplishment and become very discouraged by the lack of progress. The result is that apathy will set in.

4. TEAM COMPENSATION/REWARD SYSTEMS THAT ENCOURAGE TEAM DEVELOPMENT

One of the critical resources that will determine the long-term team success is developing a team compensation or a team recognition system that rewards team, not individual, accomplishment. If you have a compensation system or a recognition system that focuses on the individual, what does that system say about the value of teamwork in your organization? If you want your team to develop into a mature, tightly knit, cohesive group, then you must create a system that supports and motivates people to see the value of working as a team. The way in which many organizations compensate their people actually undermines teamwork and creates a competitive polarizing work group that divides and pits people

> *If you want your team to develop into a mature, tightly knit, cohesive group, then you must create a system that supports and motivates people to see the value of working as a team.*

against one another. Many old compensation models create unnecessary stress in a new team. Team members start to think to themselves, "If I truly act as a committed team member and give all my time to my teammates to make them look like superstars, they will in turn get superstar compensation when I'm left out in the cold. I'm not going to give myself to the team until I understand what is in it for me."

One of the ways that some of my clients have dealt with team compensation is to develop what is called "at-risk pay systems" for team members. For example, team members might receive 95 percent of their base pay throughout the year while 5 percent of their base pay is held in an escrow account, at risk. When the team reaches its preset goals, the team members will then get that 5 percent at risk plus a matching 5 percent as a team gain-sharing bonus. The message is very simple. If your team performs well, you as an individual will be compensated well. If your team loses, you will lose. This kind of team compensation system stresses the difference, very clearly, between casual involvement and personal commitment. Now, this is the kind of pond water treatment that allows your team to perform swimmingly!

JUST-N-TIME TRAINING

One of the key issues I want you to think about as you help your team establish its training plan is to be very careful not to overload them with interpersonal skills training, technical skills training, and administrative skills training all at the same time. Use what I call "Just-N-Time Training" when developing your team training plan. First give your team members what they most need, what they can use immediately. Do not offer training to your team that they will not use until

18 or 24 months later. This approach avoids unrealistic expectations for power and authority that the team will not receive until much later, and it also avoids wasting the team's energy. Your team members will lose what they do not use. An ancient Chinese proverb sums it up best, "I hear something, I soon forget it. I see something, I might remember. I do something, I understand. That which I am allowed to practice, I master, and that which I master, I perfect."

Accountability

The fourth and final cornerstone of true empowerment is accountability. After the organization transfers authority, insists on team member input for decisions affecting the team, and provides the appropriate resources for training, then the organization can start to hold the team accountable for its performance. In America, land of the individual, many employees and managers have difficulty subsuming the individual to the collective. This country may believe that the whole is greater than the sum of its parts, but the parts are still quite individually etched in the ego. Well, teamwork requires individual accountability as well as group accountability, and without both, the team effort will be frustrated and eventually doomed.

Three Critical Areas of Accountability

Team members will still have the ability to evaluate one another and measure each other's contributions by looking at three critical areas:

1. The individual's depth of contribution to the team. His or her expertise in one particular

area, perhaps a specialization, or a dynamic ability to do a particular job extremely well.

2. The individual's breadth of contribution to the team. His or her ability to do all the jobs in the team, to cross-train, to be flexible.

3. The individual's height of contribution to the team. Here we are talking about leadership skills, training skills, executive skills, motivational skills.

So even in a team culture, many teams will elect from their members a team MVP. Their most valuable team player is the person who has made outstanding contributions with his or her depth, breadth, and height to assist the team in accomplishing its mission. Remember, though, the individual is being rewarded for valuable team-oriented behaviors.

The 10 Characteristics of a Successful Team

I have spent 15 years working with all kinds of football teams, college teams, sport teams, executive management teams, pilot teams, surgical teams, and I've discovered that there are basically 10 characteristics that separate winning teams from those that struggle.

In the late 1950s, the Green Bay Packers of the National Football League was one of the worst teams to ever play the game. The team was so bad that players did not want to play there. Coaches from other football teams would try to motivate their own players to perform better by threatening to trade them to

Green Bay. Green Bay became known as Siberia. And no one wants to go to Siberia.

All of that changed when a coach named Vince Lombardi took over. Within three short years under Lombardi's leadership, the Green Bay Packers went from the outhouse to the penthouse by winning their first National Football League championship. Under Lombardi, the Packers became so dominant as a team that they won five championships within seven years, including a still unprecedented, unmatched three consecutive NFL championship seasons. Siberia got a new name: Title Town USA. The impact of Packer greatness was so profound that until this day, the National Football League Super Bowl Trophy is called the Vince Lombardi Trophy.

How did this team go from doormat to dynasty? When Lombardi took over the Packers in 1959, he told his struggling team that he had never been associated with a losing team, and he was not going to start now. He told them that there are all kinds of planes, and trains, and trucks, and automobiles for people to leave on if they are not going to dedicate themselves to practicing perfection. Lombardi told them that practice does not make perfect because you can practice something incorrectly, but that practicing perfection will lead to continuous progression, meaning you can always better your best.

He told his team that they would become brilliant at the basics and fantastic at the fundamentals; that they would learn to do the right things right all the time. In the early stages of their training, he focused his team's attention on mastering 10 basic plays. The entire team strategy was built around the perfect execution of these 10 basic plays. Lombardi believed that if his team could perfect these fundamentals then very few teams could ever stop the plays even when their opponents knew what was coming because, he said, very few people had that kind of commitment to greatness. He said, "It is easy to be ordinary. It is easy to be average, but it takes courage, commitment, and conviction to excel." Of the 10 plays that he built his team around, he had one that served as the cornerstone, the linchpin, that upheld the other 9. This play required exquisite timing, coordination, and collaboration to be successful. Lombardi believed that if his team could master and perfect what he called "the Power Sweep," they would be champions. The play is not confusing, or even complicated; it is very simple, yet many teams failed to perfect the coordination of individual effort required to pull it off.

What is amazing about the Green Bay Packer story, my friends, is that they were not even close to being the most talented team of their era. They had no Jim Brown. They had no Joe Namath. They had very average players, but like other great teams, they understood the power of synergy, they practiced excellence, and they worked hard.

Your 10 Plays

Successful teams like successful people have certain characteristics that separate them from the crowd and allow them to achieve success consistently. What are those characteristics?

1. Successful teams have dynamic effective leadership and support from top management. They understand that though you can barely push people across the street, you can lead them around the world. For years the old saying has been, "You can lead a horse to water, but you can't make it drink." But these

teams understand you can make people thirsty.

> *Successful teams understand that though you can barely push people across the street, you can lead them around the world.*

2. Successful teams have a shared unified vision, a sense of destiny. The team is able to describe to itself a preferred future state, to envision how a job well done will look. These teams have a sense of a clearly defined purpose. It was Margaret Thatcher who wrote, "I cannot change the past. There are people in my government who can manage the present. It is my unique responsibility as the leader of this nation to shine a spotlight into the future and then to allow my people to create that future." George Bernard Shaw once said, "You see things as they are and ask why. But I dream things that never were, and ask why not." Dr. Martin Luther King once said, "If a group of people have not found at least one thing they are willing to stand on, defend, even die for that's good, that group is not fit to lead and in some cases not fit to exist. For either we will stand for something or fall for anything."

3. Successful teams have clearly defined short-term and long-term goals that are specific and that can be measured.

4. Successful teams have quantifiable and quantitative daily objectives to help them achieve their goals.

5. Successful teams have Just-N-Time Training.

6. Successful teams have organization—authority and decision-making lines that are clearly understood by team members.
7. Successful teams appreciate the value of conflict on the team. Conflict is a fact of life and it is how one deals with it that separates winners from losers.
8. Successful teams respect each others' personal differences as a reflection of personality traits. These characteristics are understood, appreciated, and well utilized.
9. Successful teams have open communication and share resources.
10. Successful teams celebrate their success and share their failures as a team.

Teams: **T**ogether, **e**veryone can **a**chieve **m**ore!

THREE

Healthy Teams

The Sears Roebuck Tower in Chicago is a regal structure—it stands 1,000 feet in the air and sways with the wind. What many do not know is that while it is a thousand feet in the air, it is also a thousand feet in the ground. Building a towering structure on the edge of Lake Michigan means working with a soft geological foundation— sand, sandstone, and limestone. The engineers realized that they could not build this gigantic structure on this shaky ground without a solid foundation. So they had to blast away, blast away, blast away, and blast away, until they found bedrock—granite. They had to go down about a thousand feet before they ever reached bedrock, and only then could they begin to lay the foundation. That's a lot of time working down in the hole in the ground. You're pouring cement and concrete, and working with steel and iron. Yet, people on the surface will say, "What are they doing? We don't see any progress." They don't realize you cannot build a great structure without an equally great foundation.

I think the same is true for building a great team. Anybody can just throw people into a room and give them hats that look alike, a flip chart, a marker, and some notebook paper and say, "Now become a team." Then through osmosis and transcendental meditation you hope that they just evolve with a kind of synergistic cohesive click. Within a few months, of course, this team falls apart from a lack of proper training, guidance, or development. I have seen teams fail. I have seen teams succeed. The teams that

> *The teams that succeed over a long haul are the teams that spend the time laying a sure foundation.*

succeed over a long haul are the teams that spend the time laying a sure foundation. So in this chapter I'm going to talk about and share with you the laying of the foundation and other aspects of success. If you have to restart your team-building process, then do it. If you are starting from scratch, ready to begin, then do it, but do it properly. Remember that proper preparation prevents poor performance and possible punishment.

The Three Phases of Implementation

There are primarily three phases of implementing empowered teams:

> Phase 1, which will be the focus of this chapter, is called the Preparation Phase.
> Phase 2 is called the Actual Team Growth and Team Development Phase.
> Phase 3 is called the Team Evaluation Phase.

Combined, the three phases will normally take between three and four years, sometimes even five years, to move through. It's important to understand that this is not a *Trip to Bountiful* situation where your team arrives at the evaluation phase and everyone gets lunch. These phases, perhaps with some exception for the preparation phase, are places your team will go into and out of with some regularity as it embraces new employees, new tasks, or even new challenges posed by the competition. There is no top of the ladder, okay we're done, end-of-the-sentence period in team development unless the team, like an organism, dies.

It does, nevertheless, take a long time for teams to move through these phases. Why? Take a look at professional sports. How long does it take for a great coach to move a team from absolute infancy to the mountain top, to maturation? Remember our discussion about Vince Lombardi and the Green Bay Packers? It took him no less then three years to build a championship team. In the 1970s it took Don Shula three years to take a losing team, the Dolphins, to its first Super Bowl. It took Lou Holtz of the Notre Dame Fighting Irish three years. It took Jimmy Johnson and Jerry Jones of the Dallas Cowboys three years. I think you're getting my message here: Building a team is not the same as building a model airplane. The latter is a one-time project, but team building requires continuous learning, unlearning, and relearning of some very basic principles. I urge you to take your time to do it right!

Look at the Saturn Corporation. Do you know it took Saturn eight years to make a profit? I know you're saying, "Ron, I don't have eight years to turn my organization around or to implement teams." I understand that. But just so you know, Saturn is an organization that was built in a grainfield, built from scratch, with all the latest technology and people and management and a new team environment, and it took Saturn eight years to implement its team philosophy and turn a profit. All I'm saying is if you are looking for a quick fix to your problems, teams are not the solution. Teams will change the way your organization works. They will create more problems

> *If you are looking for a quick fix to your problems, teams are not the solution. Teams will change the way your organization works.*

Figure 3–1 The Roles of the Players throughout the Preparation Phase

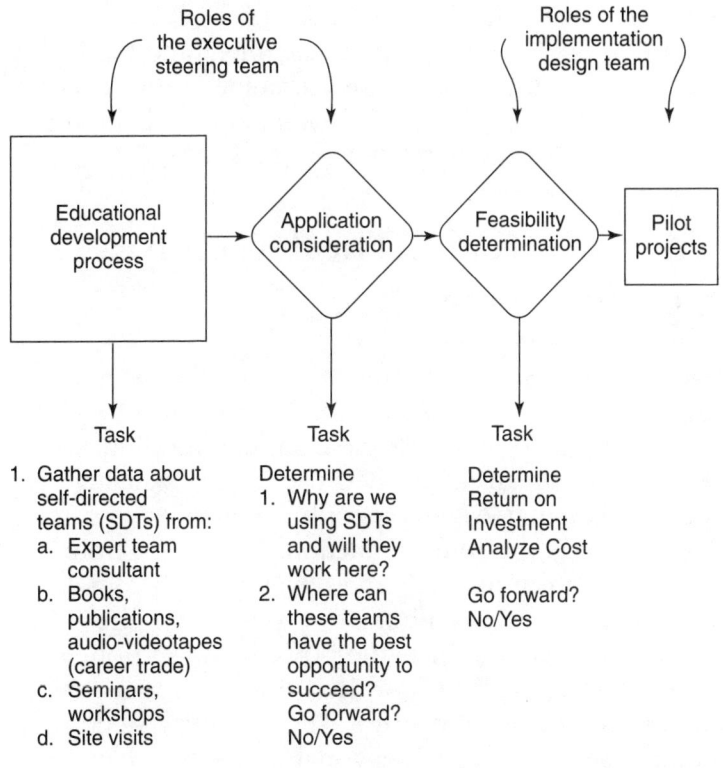

than they will solve, if you do not take time and develop them properly. Figure 3–1 shows how this all-important preparation phase should proceed.

Step One: Preparation

As I mentioned earlier, building a great building requires an equally great foundation, and that takes planning and investigation. So, we begin to build teams by doing our research. The group that does this is usually called the executive steering committee. This committee signals the seriousness of the endeavor because it is made up of key players in your organization, including top management and top union leaders. In our metaphor, this committee represents the engineer surveying the site, looking at the plans, and analyzing what problems need to be solved.

The First Team: The Executive Steering Committee

The executive steering committee is itself a team, a cross-functional, diagonal team. By cross-functional, I mean it is made up of people from different functions within your organization. Because it is an executive steering committee, these people are also leaders in the organization, from production, from sales, from marketing, from research and development, from customer service, from human resources. So, the organization should have the power brokers from as many different divisions or departments as will be affected by the team process. The executive steering committee must also be diagonal; it needs to have a representative from each of the layers within the organization, from the bottom to the top. You're going to get the front-line people involved. You're going to have to get some machine operators involved. You're going to have to get some aides involved. You're going to have to get some schoolteachers involved. You're going to go to the front line where the bullets are flying and people are diving to meet the needs of the customers, to teach the students, and to help the patients. You're going to involve the front line, from supervision, from middle-management, from executives—so this team truly represents the organization. Remember that people tend to respect and honor that which they helped to create.

The size of the executive steering committee should be limited to between 8 and 15 members. You have to have a limit; you can't have 50 people on this team. You want just enough complexity to be able to formulate consensus and build a cohesive team environment without sacrificing originality to group-think.

INVESTIGATE THE FEASIBILITY OF TEAMS

The primary role or purpose of the executive steering committee is to investigate the feasibility of empowered teams in the organization. During the first three to six months this group needs to gather materials to learn as much about team building, self-directed teams, self-managing teams, cross-functional teams, empowered teams, as they possibly can. Remember that Ghandi said, "You cannot teach what you do not know, and you cannot lead where you are not willing to go." So we recommend that the members of this team should develop an in-house team-building resource library. The more you know, the faster you will grow, and the more you learn, the more you can financially earn. I firmly believe that it is important to develop the resources so this team can ascertain just how complex is the challenge ahead of them should they decide to implement empowered teams. Your library should include books, videos, audiotapes, manuals, workbooks, case studies, reports, white papers—all kinds of information that will allow you to ascertain, at least intellectually, the benefits, the risks, and the rewards of implementing empowered teams. Einstein once said, "It is not important for a person to know every single thing, but it's absolutely imperative for them to know where they can find every single thing."

Develop Expert Knowledge

The second task that the executive steering committee must do is attend a series of training seminars and workshops—not just one series—on the following topics: how to implement empowered teams, how to lead empowered teams, the manager becoming a coach, the value of total quality leadership, how to manage diversity on a team, at-risk pay compensation, coaching and reaching consensus, how to negotiate win-win solutions, presentation skills, overcoming resistance to change, and stress management. These are some of the fundamentals we recommend that the executive steering committee become knowledgeable about so they can better understand the team-building process ahead.

Visit Other Successful Teams

A third responsibility of the executive steering committee is to become knowledgeable about how teams are working at other organizations. To this purpose, the committee should make site visits to other organizations to understand what their experience has been implementing teams. Yes, every member of your team will travel for this benchmarking visit. Does this sound expensive and time consuming? Well, it is. So is medical school, law school, or any kind of professional training. Implementing teams needs to be treated as a professional move on the part of your committee and your organization. Even though it is expensive, it is time consuming, your group must make these visits together in order to discuss and of visit may spark innovation and creativity and catalyze change within your own organization.

When you visit an organization that is using self-directed work teams or empowered teams, you want basically to ask some simple questions. One, if you could do this all over again, what would you do differently? I guarantee that 95 percent of the responses will be, "If we had a chance to do this implementation all over again, we would have spent more time in preparation. We had no idea of the complexity, of the pitfalls, of the interpersonal conflicts, of the difficulties, or of the consequences that would occur as a result of this paradigm shifting in norms and values. We would have spent more time laying a proper foundation."

THE TEAM READINESS ASSESSMENT

As part of this general preparation, the executive steering committee also must conduct an extensive team-readiness assessment to determine and identify potential barriers to implementation. You'll want to answer questions like, "What organizational structures, policies, and systems are destructive to team development and must be changed?" You must describe the organizational culture as it is and then describe how it needs to change. Is it open? Is it participative? Is it top down? Is it autocratic? You must assess resistance from management and union. Working with a facilitator, the committee will carry out three written assessments:

1. An organizational readiness assessment to ascertain the commitment level among the organization's leaders.
2. A performance gap analysis to see if leaders are willing to invest at least two years.

evaluate what you see together. Labor has to walk with management, together on purpose, to make this process work. For anyone to pretend to be the eyes and ears of another is foolishness. One more administrative note while we're talking about expenses: in some cases, depending on the size and

Implementing teams needs to be treated as a professional move on the part of your committee and your organization.

nature of your organization, temporary workers may have to be hired to fill in while committee members are their busiest. Co-workers also should expect to pitch in just as they would should someone need to respond to a family emergency or require maternity leave.

Yes, you're going on a site visit. It's common sense. Why would you want to implement a culture transformation in the organization without going out and asking people who have done it before you, "How does this team thing work, what have been your challenges, what have been your difficulties?" So I recommend—**highly**—to any organization in the midst of implementing teams or contemplating teams to schedule at least three site visits. Working with your teams implementation facilitator, who may well be an independent specialist, you will choose an organization similar to yours that has had self-directed work teams in place for at least five years—and it's working. You could also go to an organization that has used self-directed work teams or empowered teams for about five years and is struggling. And you may want to go to an organization that is totally different from yours and find out how they are using teams. This type

3. An organizationwide survey that assesses every member of the organization's level of knowledge.

The committee may conduct an organizationwide survey using an instrument similar to the one in Figure 3–2. Answers to the questions in the survey can help determine organizational readiness by assessing each person's perceptions about the organization in particular and teams in general.

This short questionnaire can be used as a net for gathering a sense of where the organization is and where it needs to go. It doesn't have one standout issue; its purpose is to show the problems that need to be addressed. For every organization priorities will be different, but each organization needs to have a system to ascertain where the barriers will be. This system helps avoid the ready-fire-aim syndrome. This questionnaire can be taken as many times by as many people as the executive steering committee deems helpful. It can be used to assess progress in weak departments or to determine an appropriate department for a pilot project.

WRITE THE FINAL REPORT

The steering committee will write a report after all their research into teams, their site visits, and their surveys. That report, delivered to the leaders of the organization (CEO, superintendent, principal) will essentially say red light, green light, or yellow light. The steering committee will decide yes, let's do it; no, not now; or let's wait awhile, or let's start smaller. If the steering committee decides to go, then its members must champion the team implementation process in a visible, tangible way. In their report the executive steering committee will document their work and show

Figure 3–2 How Ready Is Your Organization for Self-Directed Teams?

Circle one number for each statement as it applies to this inventory.

SA(4) = Strongly Agree
A(3) = Agree
D(2) = Disagree
SD(1) = Strongly Disagree

	SD	D	A	SA
1. Our management team has a history of following through in organizational changes.	1	2	3	4
2. Our employees will view self-directing teams as a cultural change rather than just a new "program."	1	2	3	4
3. Our managers are willing to take risks delegating authority and to empower employees to be self-managing.	1	2	3	4
4. Our supervisors display effective interpersonal communication skills and could serve as coaches of teams.	1	2	3	4
5. Our front-line employees are willing to be cross-trained and are willing to participate in teams.	1	2	3	4
6. Our front-line employees will view self-directing teams as a positive change rather than a negative one.	1	2	3	4
7. Our trade union will participate in the team implementation process and if necessary renegotiate job classification and work rules.	1	2	3	4
8. Our compensation system could be converted to a team compensation system.	1	2	3	4
9. Our managers and supervisors are willing to commit the resources to support self-directed teams.	1	2	3	4
10. A clear time line for the conversion to teams has been communicated to employees.				

in detail how teams will fit into the organization's vision and strategic plan. When successful implementation occurs, the successful organizations have implemented teams for a distinct purpose.

The steering committee will also draft a charter

> *When successful implementation occurs, the successful organizations have implemented teams for a distinct purpose.*

(team mission statement that relates to the overall mission of the organization) that explains the purpose and the value of teams. This charter should articulate the real strategic advantage for going with teams—not just because it's the preferred flavor of the month or because your committee has spent six months studying the idea. In essence, the question the steering committee must answer is how teams will give your organization a sustainable competitive advantage.

Figure 3–3   Hillside Rehabilitation Hospital's Mission Statement

Partners for Change Mission Statement

To be the best in rehabilitation in a state-of-the-art facility, with the ability to grow and meet the needs of the people we serve through teamwork and employee involvement resulting in pride and self-satisfaction.

Purpose

The purpose of the Hillside Labor Management Steering Committee is to create an environment with open communication, empowered employees, using the problem-solving process and team approach in decision making to ensure quality patient care and financial stability.

For Hillside Rehabilitation Hospital, whose experience with teams we'll discuss in Chapter 6, the executive steering committee's team charter shows a determination to match increasing complexities of managing health-care finances, labor costs, and technological advances with the best solutions the hospital can offer in the interest of patient wellness. The hospital realized that empowering employees and moving to a team-based environment would ensure that the organization had access to all of its human resources in solving the problems it faced (see Figure 3–3). That's sustainable competitive advantage—freeing your employees to contribute their ideas regardless of the letters that follow their name (i.e., RN, MD, and so on).

The Design Team: From Engineer to Contractor

Back to the Sears Tower for just a minute. Once the engineer has surveyed the scene and decided that, with some work, the structure could be built here, he or she turns the project over to contractors. In the case of our organization, the work now becomes the responsibility of the design team. Look again at Figure 3–1 for a picture of this part of the Preparation Phase. The design team can either be a committee of the executive steering committee or a totally separate group that gets its direction from the executive steering committee. Very often, the design team is simply an extension of the executive steering committee with very few, if any, changes in composition.

The design team is responsible for determining the specific application of empowered teams and for laying the groundwork and providing the supports to implement teamwork in the organization. The primary task of the design team is to determine and consider different approaches for implementation. The design team identifies where, within the organization, this kind of a culture transformation has the best chance of succeeding. The design team is the specific group that will actually implement a team, look at the process from a micro-perspective, and recommend an organizationwide approach. This is the team that will perform cost analysis and establish team selection and training criteria.

A PILOT PROJECT AND A SMART METHOD

The design team will recommend a selection of pilot projects to test the theories, assumptions, and data gathered by the executive steering committee. A pilot is a program or project whose purpose is to be a guinea pig—the canary in the coal mine. The pilot will reveal the kinds of problems, where extra attention needs to be paid, and how difficult the implementation of the teams will be on a wider scale in your organization. When choosing a pilot project, follow what I call the "**SMART** method":

- **S**—Make certain that the pilot project is very **specific,** and don't bite off more than you can chew. Focus on one thing you want to test, one thing you want to change, one thing you want to increase.
- **M**—Make certain that this project is **measurable:** If you cannot measure its success or failure, you've wasted your time. You want to be able to track and measure the success of this particular process, make it quantifiable, make it quantitative.
- **A**—Make certain the pilot project is **attainable** within 6 to 12 months. This is a short-term project that will allow people to work together, to iron out problems, to work out the kinks, to work out the bugs, and to accomplish something within three to six months.
- **R**—Make it **relevant** to your power brokers and to the expectations and needs of the organization, so employees notice and care. For example, reducing waiting time in the cafeteria from 30 minutes to 12 minutes is something most people will notice and care about.
- **T**—Have a clearly defined **time line** for starting and for ending. At one manufacturing facility in the Midwest only a half hour was allocated for lunch. The cafeteria was set up assembly-line style with a single cashier and one food line. The running gag was that it took 20 minutes to go

through the line, but only 10 minutes for indigestion. Morale was low, complaints were high. The design team set up a pilot team with the goal of reducing the time on the line from 15 minutes to 7 minutes. The team was given three months, a budget, and the authority necessary to make any change that would be relevant to their goal. The answer? The team replaced the assembly line system with a scramble system. Stations were set up for salad, soup, deli, and other cafeteria offerings. The time from the cafeteria door to the lunch table was reduced to 7 minutes, morale was rebuilt, and those team members felt like heroes.

Working with pilots at the beginning is a good strategy—if a pilot fails, it is easier to revisit. You're not announcing we're going to go to self-directed work teams and empowered teams, all at once throughout the whole organization. A pilot is seen as an experiment. If it succeeds—great. If it fails—that's okay too, because it was a learning process. It allows you to get some exposure to the concept in your particular organizational structure.

> *Working with pilots at the beginning is a good strategy—if a pilot fails, it is easier to revisit.*

Once the pilot project is over, the executive steering committee together with the design team will analyze the experience. You may want to do at least two or three pilots at the same time using different groups so you can get a feel of what's going on. Once you bring back the data from your pilot projects, then you must consider the organizational changes that will be necessary to support a team culture. That's where many organizations fail. They do not learn from their pilots; they don't even have pilots. They don't consider what organizational changes must be made, which they've learned from this experiment, in order to allow these self-managing, empowered teams to be able to succeed. The pilot project primarily will teach you what changes—what structures, what policies, what systems—are necessary to create healthier pond water (see Figure 3–4).

Figure 3–4

The way teams work . . .

- Top management forms a cross-functional diagonal executive steering committee to study teams and recommend an implementation strategy.
- The executive steering committee made up of top management, middle management, front-line employees, and when necessary, union representatives. It commits to a time line of three to six months to gather data about creating a successful team culture from these options:
  1. Develop an in-house team resource library of books, videotapes, and audiotapes about teams.
  2. Send employees to formal team-training workshops or hire an expert consultant who will guide this group in the implementation process.
  3. Make site visits to other successful team-based companies and cultures to get a firsthand idea of how it looks to work and manage with a successful team.

Or don't work

- A lone managerial wolf dictates the team idea downward and expects teams to develop almost by osmosis or after a one-day seminar. This manager says, "Don't worry about it. The cream rises."
- The mandate is given. The front-line employees are not involved in the decision. The threat is given to the managers, "Empower or else." No cohesive, strategic learning process is developed. One manager says, "My goodness, this isn't rocket science here, it is just team building."

(continued)

Figure 3–4 Continued

- The cross-functional executive steering committee, once it has conducted its research on the success and the feasibility of teams, forms a design team to consider implementation strategies and approaches. The design team normally includes about 8 to 10 people with the responsibility of thinking about the application of teams in their organization.
- Using questions similar to those found in Figure 3–2, the design team conducts a feasibility audit to determine implementation barriers and the return on investment.
- The design team develops a team selection and team training plan that emphasizes interpersonal skills, technical cross-training skills, and administrative skills, always using Just-N-Time training.
- The design team schedules training classes for team managers and team coaches. All attend to set a team example. The design team establishes a team compensation and team recognition plan to reinforce the value of team building among members. Several pilot teams are established to test the team system on a small scale.
- Since the union leadership was a part of the executive steering committee from the very beginning, job classification and work rules have been redesigned to better fit into the team system. Union leadership had a specifically scheduled and very productive site visit with the UAW at Saturn and the United Steelworkers at COMBOL American Brass.

- No time line is given for the conversion to a team system.

- Top management refuses to attend training classes. They send others to attend in their places. They are just too busy.

- Every department is mandated to start teaming immediately.

- Every department is mandated to start teaming immediately. Every three months a new directive, a new direction, is announced and changes are made. Top management is more reactive than proactive.

- Since the union had very little involvement from the beginning of the process, union leadership distrusts, balks, and resists all attempts to modify labor contracts in any way. Very little support comes from the union for empowered teams. Supervisors feel threatened by the so-called empowered teams. Very little training is offered on how to coach. Some supervisors actually begin to sabotage the effort. They have had very little time to prepare for the process.

(continued)

Figure 3–4 Concluded

- Company in year 2 of the teaming process has seen productivity increase, grievances decrease, customer satisfaction and ratings improve, and overall employee morale improve. The group has improved the pond water.

- After 1 1/2 years, very stressful years, the empowered team is labeled another management flavor-of-the-month flop, teams disband, and morale is at an all time low. This group ignored the pond water and the fish became sicker than ever. Management conclusion: Teams do not work.

Family, Sports, Churches, Political Parties, Business—What All Successful Teams Have in Common

I am going to share with you now the main characteristic that all successful teams—sports teams, religious teams, political teams, family teams, business teams—have in common: a good leader, a good coach. The coach is a vital part of every team—while the coach is never on the team, the coach is always for the team. The coach's role is that of educator, trainer, guide; and the coach is the single person responsible for team development. The coach may be someone you recognize from management, or a consultant hired specifically for his or her skills with team development. The coach will help the team write its mission statement and attend team meetings through the most crucial developmental stages.

> *The coach is a vital part of every team—while the coach is never on the team, the coach is always for the team.*

Most of us have known a good coach. We might have called her a mentor or known him from Little League or as our pastor. These significant leaders in our lives have very special characteristics that cause them to stand out from others.

A Good Leader Is Credible

All teams need the full support of their leaders to make the process happen. People around the coach catch the excitement, catch the enthusiasm, and catch the commitment. Successful team coaches are critical to successful teams. What I have learned in my 12 years of observing, watching, and coaching is that there are certain attributes that successful team leaders possess. The main quality is priceless, and it can be lost much more easily than it can be gained. It's credibility. A credible team-leader generates goodwill, has good sense, and is identified by his or her good character.

> *Successful teams have effective, dynamic coaches who lead by example. Their belief in an idea is so real and so strong, it becomes contagious.*

- Goodwill is revealed to team members in their belief that you are truly concerned about what they think, what they feel, and what they need. A good team-coach understands that people today do not care how much you know until they know how much you care. It is having a servant mentality. It is the power of Ghandi who understood that before you could lead, you had to serve. It is Dr. Martin Luther King going to

Memphis to help garbage workers who were on strike even though his life was being threatened. It's the Good Samaritan mind-set: "If I don't stop to help this man, what is going to happen to him?" That's goodwill.

- Good sense helps a coach meet people where they're at. Good sense directs communication; it's revealed in the talent to speak plainly and think clearly. In psychology we learn that people make decisions to change for their reasons and not your reasons. So your reasons must make good enough sense to become their reasons. You show good sense when you take the extra effort to make certain that the message that was sent out is the same as the message being received. You follow up. You understand that feedback is the breakfast of champions.

- Good character supplies the important extra mettle in the heat of the battle. It shows you how to maintain an objective, unbiased, centered outlook on issues, people, and problems. No matter how thin you slice a piece of bread, it always has two sides.

One of the coaches that had an impact on my life when I was growing up in Cleveland was the pastor of the Good Shepherd Baptist Church. I admired this man's conviction, consistency, and strength. At age 15 when I was grappling with my identity, this man took me under his wing. He taught me what it meant to be a leader. I wanted to be like him; he was my model of consistency, courage, and conviction. Although I travel over 200 days a year working with professional-sports coaches, corporate executives, and college presidents, I have never met a more dynamic, inspirational, and credible leader than I met in Eddie L. Hawkins—a true champion of goodwill, good sense, and good character.

This coach, my pastor, taught me that failure is not necessarily final. Failure is going to happen; you are going to stumble. You are going to fall, but he taught me to realize that failure is not so much the falling down as it is the lying down. He taught me that when life knocks you down, and it will, you have to find a way to land on your back because if you can look up, then you can get up. He told me that you have to be resilient. You have to be persistent.

A Good Leader Is Confident

The second quality that effective leaders possess is confidence. A successful team coach has to have confidence in himself or herself before the team can have confidence in itself. During the most difficult times, the team leader needs to be a beacon of hope and inspiration. I imagine Winston Churchill standing amid the ruins of London, the result of the Nazi Luftwaffe blitzkrieg, and saying over the radio to his fellow Englishmen, "We will never, never give up or give in to such tyranny." Churchill was no less than a beacon of hope during difficult times encouraging his people to be their best.

During a crisis, through the rough times, that's when the leader earns his or her stripes. It is easy to be a great leader when everyone likes you, productivity is soaring, money is in the bank, and your reputation is spotless. But when the rubber meets the road, nobody believes in you anymore, your friends shut you out, your own dog won't acknowledge you, that's when a leader is made. The two most important qualities are your vision, belief, and commitment to the process of building a championship team, and your ability to communicate those ideas in a shared way.

When Jerry Jones took over the Dallas Cowboys in 1989, he made one of the most unpopular decisions in football history. The Dallas Cowboys were called America's Team for their clean-cut all-American image. The leader of the Cowboys since 1960 was a God-fearing, church-going, football genius named Tom Landry. For 29 years, he had been the only coach the Dallas Cowboys had. But in the late 1980s, the luster of the Cowboy's image had begun to tarnish, they went through consecutive losing seasons. The rumor was that the modern game of professional football had passed by this old warhorse.

When Jerry Jones bought the Dallas Cowboys, he knew it was time for a change and he fired Tom Landry. The football world was shocked. The city of Dallas went berserk. The local media burned Jerry Jones electronically and in print. Jerry Jones found himself in the middle of a firestorm of negative public opinion. To make matters worse, the man that he hired to replace Tom Landry had absolutely no professional football coaching experience. He hired Jimmy Johnson, his college roommate at Oklahoma, who had won a national championship with University of Miami of Florida. Then, during their first season together, Jerry Jones and Jimmy Johnson won only one game out of 16. Fans burned their season tickets, and the media labeled Jerry "Jethro" from the old Beverly Hillbillies television show. They charged that this "Hick from Oklahoma" had come in and within one year destroyed America's Team.

To his credit, Jerry Jones never wavered, never flinched like the Cowboy he was. He sat tall in the saddle, faced his vociferous critics and said, "In three years, you people who call us fools and idiots will be calling us World Champions." He said, "We are going to plan our work, and work our plan, and in the end we will create not only a winning team, but the most profitable team in all of sports." Now that's leadership. From the ruins of a one-win season, Jerry Jones' confidence in his vision, his belief, and his commitment would not be compromised. Four years later, the Dallas Cowboys had won two consecutive titles, and in 1995 they were rated the most valuable sports franchise in the world. And in 1996, with a change to Barry Switzer, a coach with a more facilitative than directive approach to his team, they won the Super Bowl—again. The lesson here is to approach your team from where it is and give it the kind of leadership it needs.

As a coach, you are a thermostat, not simply a thermometer. A thermostat maintains the temperature. It regulates the ambiance. It keeps things steady in an ever-changing environment. A thermometer goes up and down with every failure. Your confidence, belief, vision, and passion can be contagious to your team, but so can your pessimism and your doubt. Coach of this team, if you are the only one left during this difficult time who believes that your team can win and be successful, then be the only one left. Stand for something great, build your confidence, read encouraging books, reach out and help those who are struggling, and be a resilient and persistent leader. On July 4, 1872, Calvin Coolidge said the following:

> Nothing in the world can take the place of persistence. Talent will not; nothing is more common than unsuccessful men with talent. Genius will not; unrewarded genius is almost a proverb. Education will not; the world is full of educated derelicts. Persistence and determination are omnipotent.

FOUR

Team Difficulties

Does the following sound familiar? Your team has been working together now for over 10 months. The excitement of the process is beginning to fade. Emotions like regret, frustration, apathy, and even hostility begin to cool the enthusiasm of the team and the coach alike. What appeared to be a good idea now looks like the biggest miscalculation since the Edsel and New Coke.

Your team has become a polarized, subdivided, narcissistic clique. Productivity has dropped, complaints are on the rise, and at almost every team meeting you hear the same whining:

- √ That's not my job—I was not hired to do this kind of work.

- √ That's not my problem—I took care of my responsibility.

- √ That's not my fault—I didn't do anything wrong.

- √ This team stuff is not working—let's go back to how things use to be.

The Healthy Team Test

If the scenario above sounds like one of your team meetings you have picked up the right book, and you are in the right chapter. This chapter is specifically written for teams that are experiencing the doubt and confusion that marks the storming stage, but have not given up—yet. You and your team members are still trying to create a successful team culture in spite of the obstacles and difficulties. If you are not sure where your team is, have your team members take the test in Figure 4–1 and see how you score.

Figure 4–1 How Healthy Is Your Team?

Assess the health of your team! Rate your team's health on a scale from 1 to 5, with 5 being outstanding; 1 being unacceptable.

1. Vision	Team members clearly understand why their team exists and are personally committed to achieving its mission.	_____
2. Coaching	The positions of team leader and coaches have been identified, defined, and filled with qualified and trained employees.	_____
3. Priorities	Team members know what needs to be done next by whom and by when to achieve team goals.	_____
4. Objectives	Team members understand the strategic planning process.	_____
5. Training	Team members have attended sessions for interpersonal skill development, administrative skill development, technical skill development, cross-training, and leadership development in the past six months.	_____
6. Conflict	Disagreements and problems in the team are openly dealt with and completely resolved.	_____
7. Uniqueness	Team members feel that their unique personalities are appreciated and properly blended for optimum team effectiveness.	_____
8. Empowerment	Team members have the authority to plan their work, implement their ideas, and control their work process.	_____
9. Communicate	Team members have held effective and efficient team meetings. Team decisions are reached through consensus.	_____
10. Success	Team members know clearly when the team has met with success, and they equally share in the success.	_____

Take the test individually and then collectively. We call this a checkup from the neck up, your quarterly physical, and it can be used on a macro- and micro-level to help you see how things are going. This quiz serves as a pointer to symptoms, not causes, and as such offers a point of departure for identifying any problems that need attention. So, if you scored 3 or below in any area, you need to discuss with your team how that area can be improved. On a macro level, you could say that

> 45–50 is great.
> 39–44 is very good.
> 35–38 is good.
> 29–34 is fair.
> 28 and fewer points is poor.

Teams have had great success using this test as an indicator of their health and well-being.

The Five Stages of Team Development: A Road Map

We would really like to think that our development is linear, that we progress on and on and on to ever greater levels of wisdom, and if we don't progress then something is wrong. Or perhaps more honestly, if *you* don't progress this way then something is wrong. I agree that the optimal life voyage is one on which we travel to greater levels of understanding and wisdom. But the trip is not linear. It more nearly resembles a telephone cord, and it can get very snarly.

We need to look at team development in a similar way—a team is, you will remember, an organism made up of living and breathing individuals. The team has stages of maturation that are attained only by hard work and experience. The hard work and experience happen in a daily, weekly, monthly grind

> *The team has stages of maturation that are attained only by hard work and experience.*

Figure 4–2   Five Stages of Self-Direction

Macro Team Maturation Scale

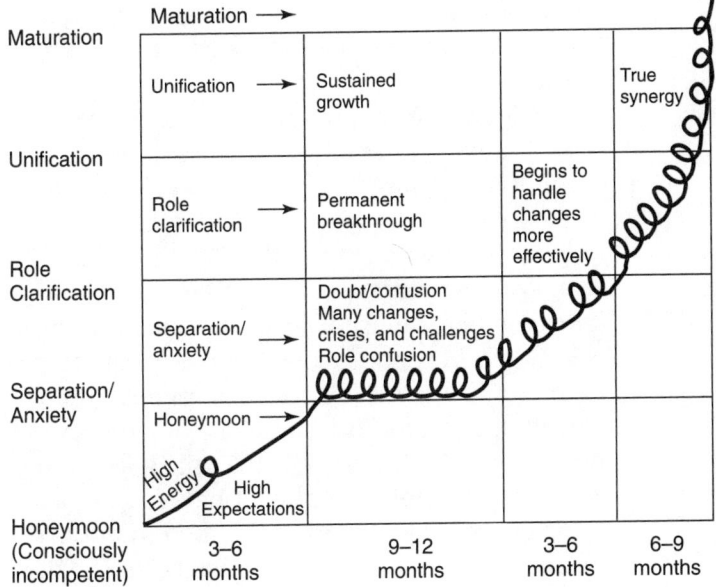

that is itself a developmental loop. This grind happens continually while the team is going through its stages—this is one reason why a good coach is so vital to team development. The Macro Team Maturation Scale in Figure 4–2, is the longer view of team development encompassing a three- to five-year period. The five stages of team development are described below.

1. ***Stage One:*** the Honeymoon Stage (also known as the Forming Stage). This stage normally lasts between three and six months. It is a stage of enthusiasm, energy, and high expectation. At this stage people on the team will say: "Who cares if the horse is blind—load the wagon, we can make it." "Let's get in the

rowboat. Let's chase Shamu and bring along the tartar sauce. We are going to have lunch today." The team believes blindly that they will boldly go where no team has gone before. It is the easiest time for team development.

2. ***Stage Two:*** the Doubt and Confusion Stage (also known as the Storming Stage). This stage is the longest, most difficult, and most taxing. This stage will last between 9 and 12, and maybe as long as 18 months. This is where many of the teams are when they call in consultants for help or give up in frustration. It is a time when productivity may dip, anxiety is high, conflict is on the rise, complaints are constant, and attitudes are characterized by pessimism, doubt, and confusion. Before there is a breakthrough you almost have a breakdown. Take for instance the experience of Chuck Yeager just prior to his breaking the sound barrier. The extreme pressure built up in his plane, and he felt it throughout his body. His plane vibrated as if it would fly apart, making every nut, bolt, and screw shake. Yet the plane held together, passed through the sound barrier, and into a new equilibrium. The danger for team members is that they will quit during the shaking, jostling, quaking of the Storming Stage.

3. ***Stage Three:*** the Role Clarification (or the Norming Stage). People begin to understand what their team roles are going to be. This phase will last between three and six months. Stage Two is the beginning of a breakdown; Stage Three is the beginning of a breakthrough.

4. **Stage Four:** the Unification Stage (also known as the Conforming Stage). People begin to conform to group ideals and goals. This stage will last between six and nine months.

5. **Stage Five:** the Maturation Stage (also known as the Empowering or the Self-Managing Stage). This is an ongoing, continuous improvement process.

In Figures 4–3 and 4–4 you can see the microdevelopment issues clearly and how they evolve throughout the team's life, which is made up of new challenges, new members, major changes, crises, and so on. The forming, storming, norming, and performing stages represent those microstages of coming together (forming), facing the anxiety of performance demands (storming), settling role and task issues (norming), and getting the job done (performing). The challenge of team building is that this cycle never goes away. As long as the team faces change, challenges, and crises, this cycle will repeat itself. The key is not to avoid the storming loop, but to recover from it more quickly. That is what team growth and maturation yields— performance—the ability to move through the early stages efficiently and then get the job done.

> *The key is not to avoid the storming loop, but to recover from it more quickly. That is what team growth and maturation yields— performance—the ability to move through the early stages efficiently and then get the job done.*

Figure 4–3 Micro Team Development Loop

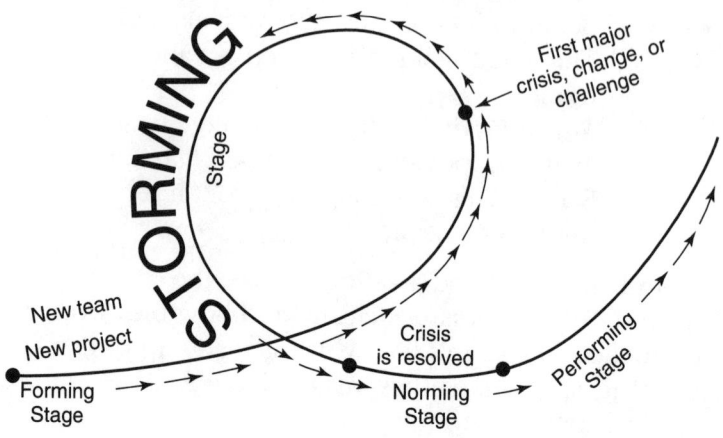

Figure 4–4 The Cycle Repeats with Each Change

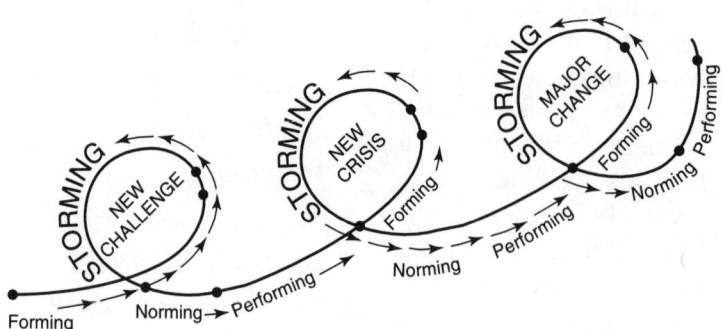

Teams that fail to mature spend more of their time, resources, and energy in the storming loop and confuse activity with accomplishment. A team that is failing will find itself stuck in the separation anxiety stage because of its inability to shorten the storming loop. If a self-managing team is unable to get out of separation anxiety within 9 to 12 months, that team is destined to self-destruct because team members are not able to break through their individualistic (narcissistic) habit to the concept of we-the-team. The key elements in the growth process that were probably unavailable to this failing team are effective coaching, strong internal team leadership, a clear mission, and a focused training program.

One other element that can result in a failed team is bad chemistry. Every team needs the right mix of people with the appropriate complement of skills in order to succeed. In each of these stages of team development, people exhibit individual characteristics, attributes, problems, and growing pains. Teams, because they are made up of people, will reflect at least all the difficulties and unresolved conflicts that we deal with individually on a daily basis. In teams the pressure is to perform together, to say less of me and more of we. None of us is more important than all of us. Soft-skill issues, interpersonal skills such as listening or negotiating, will destroy a team—it is not an issue of professional ability, it's the interpersonal

> *Teams, because they are made up of people, will reflect at least all the difficulties and unresolved conflicts that we deal with individually on a daily basis.*

stuff. As a living organism, a team during its early stages of growth needs the same kind of support, training, guidance, and direction as a child. If a team is built on a rocky foundation, deprived of the kind of support it needs to grow strong, this team will self-destruct and implode.

What are the issues that, if not dealt with in the preimplementation stage of team development, will lead to a situation in which the team fails to jell and unify? From my research and practical experience, I have identified five reasons why teams fail.

Five Ways to Fail

ONE—POOR FOUNDATION

The first and foremost reason is lack of support and guidance from top management to create an implementation strategy that will support team development. You see, your organization is either an incubator for developing teams—warming them, allowing them time to grow—or it is an incinerator—a very hot, uncomfortable, disingenuous situation that creates a self-destructive environment in which the team burns out. Which one do you have?

The first and foremost reason is lack of support and guidance from top management to create an implementation strategy that will support team development.

In an incubator, the organization understands that a team is an organism that needs the proper environment to grow. In an incinerator, the organization just throws people into the tank and hopes that something comes out.

Two—Mistrust

The second reason teams fail is because employees mistrust management motives. These employees see empowered teams as a way to ask them to do more for nothing as a ploy to downsize and to make employees do more with fewer people. In order to overcome the barriers that can lead to team failure, the organization must allow, and even encourage, employee input in the design and implementation of empowered teams. As discussed in Chapter 3, the organization should include rank-and-file employees on the executive steering committee. However, if it is too late for that, then management needs to openly acknowledge the problem. Build trust by including the employees in the process and allowing more clarity about motives.

> *In order to overcome the barriers that can lead to team failure, the organization must allow, and even encourage, employee input in the design and implementation of empowered teams.*

The executive steering committee must make certain that your organization's team implementation process is based on a solid vision, purpose, and commitment to improve working conditions for the employees. It's the committee's responsibility to make certain that top management communicates this vision to your employees. The committee should hold employee meetings so employee fears and concerns about layoffs and how compensation on teams will be handled can surface. Those fears need to be handled directly and honestly.

Three—Muddy Path

The third reason teams fail is because people are not clear about what is expected from them in the new process. Managers do not know what is expected of them, supervisors are confused about their new role, and team members are confused about what they are supposed to do and how they are supposed to do it. In order to overcome these pitfalls, the design team must help managers and team members work out the answers to the following questions:

> *The third reason teams fail is because people are not clear about what is expected from them in the new process.*

1. What is my job now?
2. How has my job changed?
3. What are the new rules?
4. What is expected of us?
5. How will we be evaluated?

Develop a list of short-term and long-range responsibilities that the team will be assuming. Develop a long-range strategic plan that clarifies these concerns:

1. How long the move to teams will take.
2. How quickly responsibilities will be transferred.

3. What support will be provided during this change process.

You must as a manager let everyone know about the risks and the possible rewards in the process.

Four—Fear of Change

The fourth reason why teams fail is the fear of change. Teams that fail do not share a vision that clearly depicts life in a team system. It is important to share up-front details on pay and reward changes that will accompany the move to teams and provide stress management courses for those taking part in this very stressful change process.

> *The fourth reason why teams fail is the fear of change. Teams that fail do not share a vision that clearly depicts life in a team system.*

Five—The Toxic Person Syndrome

The fifth and final reason teams fail is because managers tend to reward, or at least recognize, those whom we call the toxic people. You see, whenever you organize people for any significant change effort, such as implementing teams, they will fall out into a 20–60–20 bell curve.

Twenty percent of your people are going to be very excited, very inspired, and very motivated. They have been waiting for years to work in this kind of environment. They may have come from a team-based workforce, or they've read about teams, or they value the team concept. Regardless of the reason, they are willing and ready to participate and take risks. The 20 percent on the other end of the curve are those we call toxic people. These chronic whiners, moaners, doomsayers, voice some version of the following litany: "This is not going to work. We are not going to make it. It can't happen here. We have too much bad history. I can't stand you. You can't stand me. We are all going to die. It is not going to work." Now, we all have bad days, but every day? Toxic people will sabotage the process by refusing to consider the possibility of success or by refusing to be motivated by any rewards for changing their behavior. Those people in the middle we'll call the Neutral Sixty. These are the people who will carry you to success or failure, depending on how you lead the team.

The problem is that most supervisors, or team leaders, spend way too much time trying to change the behavior of the Toxic Twenty. These managers have forgotten the Positive Twenty and the Neutral Sixty. They're basically weighing their success by whether they can swing the Toxic Twenty. It's a situation that reminds me of a story about the mailman delivering mail. He walks along by old homes on dusty roads with gravel driveways, each with its mailbox. One of the houses across the street on his route has a big old hound dog sitting on the porch—long brown body, long ears, kind of wrinkled-up face. Every so often the hound will raise his big old head and just let out a big whine, "Arooh!" This goes on every half hour or so, and so the mailman keeps going down the road. He comes back to the house. The dog has not moved. Every now and again the mailman hears him howl. The mailman knocks on the door, and he asks the owner, "Sir, not to be imposing or nosy or even irritating, but what is wrong with your dog? He sits in the same spot, and he just howls all day. What is wrong with him?" The owner of the dog walks out the screen door onto the porch and turns to the right and says, "Oh, you mean old Rusty? He's all right. He's just sitting on a nail, but he is too lazy to move because it doesn't hurt enough. He just wants to whine about it." Toxic people, like that old dog, are content where they are at: they don't want to change; they don't want to see things differently. The hurt they know is better than the hurt they don't know.

Imagine, then, the situation that develops when the manager and the group spend most of their time trying to move the toxic people off that nail. Nothing could be farther from the team's mission, and there are few strategies that will end up being more enervating than this exercise in futility. For too long the paradigm of many organizations has been "the squeaky wheel gets the grease," but today in changing environments those squeaky wheels get replaced. The smart manager will focus on the energy of the Positive Twenty to motivate his or her Neutral Sixty and get the team going on its tasks. The majority of team members will begin to work and one of two things are likely to occur:

> *For too long the paradigm of many organizations has been "the squeaky wheel gets the grease," but today in changing environments those squeaky wheels get replaced.*

1. The 80 percent will first try to draw the toxic people in. They will say, "Come on. Give it a shot. This thing is working." If you can tie compensation or recognition factors to team performance, then they will see these people as being barriers to their own success.

2. If these 80 percent cannot draw the toxic people in through peer pressure and organizational behavior, they will simply drive these people out. They will let them know that when a paradigm changes either you are on the way or you are in the way. Those who say it cannot be done had better get out of the way of those who are doing it.

The Toxic Twenty will either catch on, or they will need to be moved on.

Letting Go So the Team Can Grow

There's one more big problem with empowering teams and achieving success. Managers need to understand authority differently than they have understood it in the past. Whether a team needs to accomplish particular tasks, to find a solution to a nettlesome problem, or to assess various strategies, that team must assume responsibility for its functions. A team that has no authority, has no responsibility, and vice versa. Furthermore, the reach of its authority must parallel its responsibility. You can't in good management conscience ask someone to do something and not give them the authority to do what needs to be done, can you? The process is the same for teams. After all the training, when you know they have the skills, there comes the moment when you have to let them do the work they've been assigned.

> *A team that has no authority, has no responsibility, and vice versa.*

Letting go can be hard to do. For managers who struggle with this authority issue I offer the following Four-Step Strategic Empowerment Initiative. This is a process by which the manager can ease into his or her new role as coach. It's a role with much power, much responsibility, and potentially great rewards, but it does take some learning to get it right. These four steps can help a manager systematically transfer the keys to their teams.

Step One

We ask the managers to keep and maintain a daily activities log for 30 consecutive days. In the log the managers record their daily decisions, what meetings they attended and why, what monies were spent and why, what decisions were made on specific issues and why, how crises were resolved, how responsibilities were handled. After 30 days, the manager takes this log to his or her team and shares it with them. This will accomplish two things:

1. It will help team members empathize and develop trust for what this manager has to deal with regularly—this is the beginning of the process of partnership. This process can be especially awesome for the manager who is in the position of speaking to his or her employees as if they were equals for the first time.
2. It will get the manager working with his or her team. The team and its leader can identify some very basic and fundamental responsibilities and powers that can be assumed by the team immediately, as in *today*.

Some basic responsibilities I have suggested to managers that they might want to give up:

- Scheduling work. Let the team start handling their own work scheduling. Who comes in on

Monday? Who works first shift? Who works second shift? Let them reach consensus as a team regarding how the work will be covered.

- Planning team meetings. Let the team members decide when they will meet and how long they will meet. Let them be responsible within certain parameters for planning their own meetings.
- Tracking productivity.
- Determining training needs.
- Doing team needs-assessments and evaluating their progress as a team.
- Writing reports.
- Developing a budget for team supplies.
- Scheduling vacations.
- Developing the team mission, vision, and goals statements.
- Developing a team problem-solving process.
- Conducting a workplace analysis to see what tasks are compatible with a team-oriented system.

Step Two After 30 days, the manager again meets with the team to identify future responsibilities that the team will assume in the next 12 to 18 months as the team demonstrates the three Cs of competence, confidence, and consistency in handling the responsibilities assumed from Step One. Some future responsibilities that teams might look forward to are

- Developing a peer evaluation system that makes up one-third of the annual review and reflects the team perception of the employee's ability to work in their team and the employee's level of contribution to the team's overall success.
- Becoming acquainted with suppliers and customers.

- Planning a benchmarking trip, including assigning debriefing reports when back home.
- Interviewing and selecting future team members.
- Establishing team performance incentives.
- Establishing with management a team gain-sharing program.
- Developing training programs for new employees.
- Coordinating work flow.

Step Three The coach will serve as team leader and as coach. After this point in the process, about two or three months in, we ask the manager to define the role of the newly created position of team leader and select from the team its first leader. The manager appoints the team leader in the beginning because a newly formed team may not know its members well enough to make that decision. An inexperienced team will also need to learn what kinds of skills their team leader needs. Subsequent team leaders will be chosen by the team. The team leader's responsibilities will include attending management meetings, handling interpersonal conflicts, maintaining area records, documenting team development and troubleshooting, facilitating, coordinating, making peace, and acting as a conduit between the coach and the team.

Step Four The manager identifies his or her role as the coach and clearly explains to the team what responsibilities and what powers belong to the coach. Such a list might include responding to intracompany complaints, handling disciplinary problems, preparing annual budgets, long-term strategic planning, and of course, keeping the team on track and evaluating team performance.

This incremental plan works for managers who need to get into the water one step at a time.

Remember, the successful team process takes time to do well because what is involved is change, and change for human beings does not have an automatic on and off switch—not if it is authentic. The teams also will benefit from this process because it will help members gauge management's sincerity. Seeing that the boss is willing to learn what he or she clearly needs to learn in order to successfully implement teams can be a most powerful convincer that this team process is real. Everyone needs to learn, or be reminded from time to time, that the team on top of the mountain did not fall there. Coach, by the yard it's hard, but by the inch it is a cinch.

> *Remember, the successful team process takes time to do well because what is involved is change, and change for human beings does not have an automatic on and off switch—not if it is authentic.*

FIVE

Hillside Rehabilitation Hospital: Management and Unions Team Up for a Better Way

The health-care industry today faces many of the same challenges that the U.S. auto industry faced in the late 1970s and early 1980s: overwhelming complexity, increasing competition, and accelerated change. Ford, GM, and Chrysler were forced to reinvent themselves and their management philosophies in order to survive and thrive in a cost- and quality-conscious marketplace. Health-care practitioners, hospitals, and even insurance companies are realizing that quality, cost, and customer service will separate the winners from the whiners, the pretenders from the contenders, and the champs from the chumps.

With all the proposed changes to Medicaid and Medicare looming and with insurance companies limiting reimbursement, health-care administrators are frantically looking for ways to keep their facilities afloat. Uncertainty is rife in the industry, making long-term strategic planning difficult. Suddenly, the old paradigms relating to health care and payment for services are being challenged and rewritten, almost on a daily basis. The only thing

> *Health-care practitioners, hospitals, and even insurance companies are realizing that quality, cost, and customer service will separate the winners from the whiners, the pretenders from the contenders, and the champs from the chumps.*

that looks like a sure bet in health care these days is that the pressure to reduce costs and the demand for measurable quality service will increase.

At the Hillside Rehabilitation Hospital, the need for change led to the development of cross-functional, self-directed teams whose goal it was to increase employee involvement in quality improvement efforts while at the same time reducing costs. Bill O'Connor, Hillside's CEO, has helped create an organizational culture that fosters employee involvement and accountability on every level. He believes that it is the role of management to lead by example, to follow the suggestions of "front-line partners in progress," and to step aside and allow the employees to do their work. He is a visionary who firmly believes that self-directed cross-functional teams and accountability are the initial steps for successful health-care facilities.

At Hillside, self-directed teams are on the rise, but it was not always that way.

The Background

Hillside Rehabilitation Hospital is a county-owned facility with a proud history of over 60 years of providing health-care services to a tri-county area located approximately 70 miles southeast of Cleveland. Since 1929, when the Trumbull County commissioners opened a 48-bed facility for the treatment of tuberculosis "way out in the farm country of Howland Township," this hospital's mission has changed from treating tuberculosis to treating children and adults experiencing a variety of illnesses and injuries, including stroke, head and spinal cord injury, neuromuscular disease, joint replacement, and more.

Along with physical rehabilitation, Hillside offers comprehensive alcohol and chemical dependency rehabilitation. The Addiction Recovery Center of Hillside (ARCH) program provides detoxification, acute substance abuse rehabilitation, and after care on an inpatient and outpatient basis.

While Hillside still sits on the same 28 acres of rolling wooded land that helped make it a successful sanitarium, everything around the hospital has changed dramatically. In 1995 the state of Ohio relaxed the "certificate of need" regulations that had given Hillside a monopoly on rehabilitation services in the area. Essentially, Hillside's patients had been supplied from two primary feeder hospitals. Now because of changes in state regulations, hospitals that used to send their rehabilitation patients to Hillside can develop their own rehabilitation programs, and some of them are. As a consequence, the 93-bed comprehensive rehabilitation hospital faces competition for the first time in its history. Hillside's most acute problem is its high cost of care, with labor costs being the biggest culprit. Hillside has a staff of 480, and many of them are members of the Association of Federal, State, County and Municipal Employees (AFSCME) and the Ohio Nurses Association (ONA).

Union-Management Relationship

To understand Hillside's progress today, you must understand where the hospital has come from. Its culture was born of the labor-management strife in Trumbull County, which is located in the heart of steel- and automobile-manufacturing country.

According to Deborah Bindas, president of AFSCME Local 2288,

> The labor-management climate at Hillside from 1980 through 1991 could be likened to a war zone. Each side waited for the other to attack. Many times the tactics were similar to guerrilla warfare. Workers believed they had no input or control over their jobs, job descriptions, or working conditions. Although a bargaining agreement existed, we had a difficult time enforcing the issues outlined in the contract.

Steel giants like Republic Steel, LTV Steel, and Copperweld were located in Trumbull County; Packard Electric and GM are major employers. Youngstown, Ohio, is just down the road from the hospital. During the recession of the 1970s, this area boasted one of the highest unemployment rates in the country. Because of the many plant closings in the late 1970s and early 1980s, this region of the country was widely known as the "Rust Belt." Huge, empty factories were left idle and decaying. Many families saw their jobs leave, never to return, or else spent months of every year laid off. Due to these plant closings and layoffs, an extremely adversarial and often militant work culture developed and infused many nonmanufacturing institutions with its anger and mistrust. Children grew up hearing the war stories at the dinner table about labor-management struggles. Battle lines were drawn and family and friends had to pick sides: labor or management. There was no in-between. It is in this context that the attitudes of the Hillside labor force and management team were nurtured. The situation was a powder keg awaiting a spark.

During the 1980s, the relationship between Hillside labor and management was at an all-time low, matching as it did the battles being fought by labor and management in Youngstown and elsewhere. An average of 432 grievances, more than one per day, were filed each year. Job actions and an outbreak of the blue flu, when different departments took specific days off, occurred. In most cases, these grievances and job actions were the result of lack of communication and trust or a manifestation of the extreme anxiety people felt. The grievances most often revolved around scheduling issues, days off or days on. If labor and management had been able to talk to one another, many of the grievances would never have been lodged. Sometimes the temperature rose to potential crisis levels. For example, one nurse remembers the day she and several of her peers prepared all the meals for their patients because the dietary department had shut down the kitchen by walking off the job. One day many of the nurses called in sick. Deborah Bindas emphasized,

> These were not bad people but rather they were good people who were tired of feeling mistreated. In many cases, the job actions and the blue flu were results of the pent-up frustration of not being listened to by management.

A vicious circle had developed in which management didn't listen to the union because the union would not talk to management. To call Hillside a divided camp would be an understatement. During the 1980s, the concept of teamwork between labor and management did not exist. Hillside had a monopoly with a guaranteed customer base—its feeder hospitals—and a strong cash flow. Nobody thought about the need to control costs or to be customer focused. The prevailing attitude was "When you are the only game in town, why change?" Since there were no real concerns regarding survival coming from the outside, there was no force to challenge the culture of mistrust on the inside.

The primary problem plaguing Hillside during this period was that some management leaders were bent on maintaining the status quo of the command-and-control leadership style. They wanted their departments to snap into line and do what they were told, whether it was in the bargaining agreement or not. The front-line workers felt neither respected nor valued as partners in the process, but instead saw themselves as pawns to be manipulated at the whim of the organization. At the same time, the union enjoyed one of the highest payrolls in the state of Ohio. As a county-run facility with little or no competition, the fat was there and the union greased the skillet. Self-serving and almost narcissistic, it resisted almost any effort to look at ways to improve efficiency and productivity.

During the late 1980s some efforts were made to foster better communications between labor and management. The first real labor and management team was assembled with the purpose of finding a better way of doing business. A 12-member steering committee, including both labor and management, conducted several site visits to other organizations where effective team concepts had improved labor-management communication.

This steering committee, charged with developing a plan by early 1990 to create more teams throughout the hospital, met twice a month for six months. "The concept failed for several reasons," recalled Bindas. "First, the new CEO displayed a general lack of commitment to the process of empowerment." In addition, although the new CEO had been urged by the board of trustees to sanction the program, because of his personal management style, very little authority was ever transferred to front-line employees. Finally, union members viewed the steering committee team process with suspicion. They saw it as an attempt to override the collective bargaining process and nullify the power of the contract. The union members were willing to trust **their own** leadership and buy into the concept if they did. The end result: no progress and the departure of yet another CEO.

In late 1990, a new CEO, Bill O'Connor, the sixth CEO in 10 years, took the helm of Hillside's troubled ship. With this change, representatives from the administration met with union leadership to discuss the challenges of health care in general and the challenges facing Hillside specifically. An executive leadership team also met on a monthly basis to formulate strategies to improve relations with labor. As O'Connor saw it:

> I am a firm believer that you can't do things to people, you must find a way to do things *with* people. Allowing employees to take charge of change makes for a smooth transition.

In spite of the goodwill developed between management and labor, the challenges O'Connor foresaw hit. Rising costs, decreasing reimbursement, and health-care reform resulted in a major restructuring, which led to layoffs. One would think that with the restructuring and layoffs, an extremely adversarial relationship would have redeveloped between management and the unions; but, surprisingly, just the opposite occurred.

AFSCME leadership recognized that labor relations had to change as the health-care industry was changing. They decided they had to secure Hillside's place as a rehab facility of the future. According to Marijo Shuntich, clinical program manager:

Sometimes the greatest unifier in the world is an outside threat. We all began to realize that if we didn't get our act together and start working as a team, we might not be around to argue at all.

The first area the combined leadership team looked at was the grievance procedure. An employee filed a grievance with the department head, who then responded to the complaint. Often, the union didn't accept that response and pushed the grievance through the process until it reached the board of trustees. This was a lengthy process that had a negative impact on employee morale and attitude.

Both management and the union wanted to reform the grievance process. Both believed that a real and lasting change starts on the inside and works its way out. O'Connor explained:

> If one of our priorities is to make our external customers feel important, we must first create systems and ground rules that make our internal customers feel important. Part of our strategic vision for Hillside was to change the company culture. Employees and staff had habitually distrusted and fought against whatever management said or shared. It is administration's job to create an atmosphere where every employee becomes a leader and to foster a mind-set that says *none of us is more important than all of us, including administration.*

The First Team Victory

The one idea management shared with the Hillside family that truly started to change things was the concept of **accountability.** Beginning in 1992, employees became accountable for their own actions, accountable for the things that went *right* as well as those things that went wrong. Being accountable forces people into change: When an individual knew he was going to be held responsible for a situation, his level of commitment tended to increase.

> *Employees became accountable for their own actions, accountable for the things that went right as well as those things that went wrong.*

The end result was the addition of an unwritten step to the grievance procedure: the **talking stage.** When an employee believed she had a grievance, her labor representative went to her supervisor and openly talked over the situation. With management empowering the supervisors and department managers, and the union willing to talk, the problem was most often resolved at this stage. A more responsive system had been created, one that included front-line workers in the decision process and placed fewer layers between those workers and the decision makers.

Dramatically, the grievance rate was reduced to zero within a year of implementing this talking stage!

With this success, the union leadership and management worked to develop a cooperative team relationship. The team focused its attention on providing the necessary training tools that would allow a team-oriented system to thrive. Initially the focus was on educating and training key employees on the value and the importance of working in a team environment. The leadership team selected training courses on such hot topics as organizational communications, problem solving, and conflict resolution. In groups of 16, the first wave of 64 employees went off-site to train with the Packard Electric Cooperative Effort.

During this planning and preparation stage of team development, something happened that catalyzed the change process for all Hillside employees. The hospital levy went up for renewal and was publicly attacked by a political action group in the area. For the first time in Hillside's history, all employees banded together and became one dynamic team—very motivated because someone on the outside had challenged the hospital's need for that levy. For once, everyone had a common vision and became a team as an organization.

At a board meeting in February of 1993, an unbelievable number of union members and managers came to defend the hospital. This unusual show of a united front demonstrated to the community the staff's commitment to become the best facility in the valley. During the meeting that night the light came on in Hillside's collective head as management and the union became aware that teamwork was the key to their future success.

Shortly after this team victory, another crisis tested the team concept at Hillside. During the spring of 1993, Hillside experienced financial difficulties due to low census and falling reimbursement, again making layoffs a real possibility. Once again, the power of teamwork and union commitment made a huge difference. Rather than

A more responsive system had been created, one that included front-line workers in the decision process and placed fewer layers between those workers and the decision makers.

following the usual mandatory layoff procedure based on seniority, the union suggested an innovative, voluntary, week-at-a-time layoff. The concept was so successful it would have taken a year just to schedule everyone who put in a request. Within four weeks enough people had signed on that others had to be turned away from taking time off without pay!

The message was clear. For the first time, front-line workers felt like true partners in the decision-making process.

The message was clear. For the first time, front-line workers felt like true partners in the decision-making process.

At this point, Hillside Rehabilitation Hospital labor relations took a 180-degree turn from their turbulent past. The hospital's dynamic leadership team, along with union buy-in and collaboration on decisions affecting the organization's future, has turned Hillside into a model of labor-management team success.

Local union officials receive release time, and while still on the clock, work on cross-functional team assignments. According to one of AFSCME's leadership:

> It was great. Management invested in our education, both personally and professionally. Our cross-functional executive leadership team worked together to redesign the workplace, to rewrite job descriptions, and to find more ways to empower the front-line employee to learn broader technologies and to make decisions. The most important lesson that the union learned is that self-directed teams allowed members to

work smarter, not just harder, and that made the organization more effective and viable. Teamwork enhanced our job security.

By 1995, Hillside had progressed from an adversarial, hate-filled labor-management relationship to a leadership team that has empowered its employees by giving them some control over their jobs and the methods they use to provide services to Hillside's customers. Hillside is not a utopia—setbacks have occurred and differences still exist—but the methods Hillside uses to settle conflicts have changed immensely.

Hillside had progressed from an adversarial, hate-filled labor-management relationship to a leadership team that has empowered its employees by giving them some control over their jobs and the methods they use to provide services to Hillside's customers.

Presently some 60 employees drawn from labor and management have been trained to work on various cross-functional self-directed teams and are meeting monthly to tackle work-related issues. "It is refreshing to be able to share openly and authentically one's feelings and perceptions about making Hillside a better place to work," shared one employee.

A final example of success in the new labor-management team relationship is illustrated by the use of cross-functional teamwork to solve problems arising from the 1995 contract negotiations with AFSCME.

Both sides went into negotiations with a completely different attitude than the mistrust that had colored previous contract negotiations. Instead of each side being determined to win at any cost, both sides were dedicated to win-win bargaining. Instead of bargaining until the deadline hour, the labor and management negotiators chose, as a team, to discuss the contract in four sessions. In these sessions, every item was settled without the win-lose scenario so common in past contract negotiations.

Designing the team-building process requires a long-term commitment from both management and labor as well as a willingness to support workers who are risking change. If either views the implementation of self-directed teams as nothing more than a new suggestion-box program, the process will fail. Will there ever be total buy-in from all personnel? Probably not. The reality is that there will always be those few who do not choose to participate, who are not interested, or who simply do not believe in the concept. However, that will not stop the process from taking hold and succeeding. With strong commitment from both labor and management, anything can be achieved. As the management and labor team at Hillside Rehabilitation Hospital discovered:

Designing the team-building process requires a long-term commitment from both management and labor as well as a willingness to support workers who are risking change.

Together **E**veryone **A**chieves **M**ore!

Specific Examples of Hillside's Team Success

Although problem solving through teams is still relatively new to Hillside, it has already resulted in several accomplishments.

One team, named New Start, began analyzing why and how patients arrived late to therapy or missed therapy altogether. Late or missed therapy meant decreased revenues, not to mention the fact that patients were not receiving the number of sessions Hillside promised them. With the addition of expanded therapy hours and a hospitalwide campaign for wheelchair users called "Don't Look Me Over," significant results were obtained. The purpose of the "Don't Look Me Over" wheelchair campaign was to alert all employees and volunteers of their contribution to patient transport and to the cost of missed or late sessions. In four short months, the number of sessions missed was decreased by 30 percent.

In dollars and cents, the program recouped an average of $7,000 per month from lost revenue. New Start continues to look at further improving the process until no patients miss therapy except for a medical reason. After their first-quarter results, recognition snack breaks were provided to all the staff and volunteers involved for their efforts.

Another team, named Think Pink, addressed the issue of patient falls. Falls are high-risk events for any health-care organization, and at a rehabilitation hospital where ambulating and independence are encouraged they constitute a special problem. The color pink is the hospital's color to identify safety issues. Hillside's Nursing Department developed a "patient at risk for falling" assessment tool several years ago; however, according to hospital statistics, it had little impact on actually reducing the number of patient falls. In 1993, the fall rate was at or above threshold in eight months; in 1994, for nine months. The team, which consisted of several departments and all levels of staff, discussed and looked at many issues and decided that the current assessment tool was good, but it needed to be modified and implemented hospitalwide. Therefore, the assessment tool, policies and procedures, and patient-family education were revised and an aggressive two-week safety awareness program was conducted. By August of 1995, the threshold had been exceeded only once, in January. This is another example of staff involvement bringing ownership and commitment to a process they have developed.

A final example of team performance has to do with customer service. As a part of Hillside's program evaluation, a three-month postdischarge phone call is made to approximately 10 percent of all patients who have been discharged to their homes. In addition to asking the patients about their functional status, they are asked "What could we have done to make your stay better?" By the end of January 1994, the number of patient complaints averaged about 15 per month. Hillside decided to put together a team to address the numerous and often-repeated complaints. The team listed the top seven complaints and recruited staff members to participate in a "creative production" to increase awareness and educate staff on exceptional customer service.

The creative production resulted dramatically in *The Final Insult*. The stage was set, the crowd quiet but expectant. The scent of popcorn permeated the air. A telephone rang out, signaling the beginning of a follow-up call to a former patient. In seven skits, the team (Hillside Players) re-created actual comments from former patients, communicating the frustration, anger, and even embarrassment patients sometime experienced because of staff actions and reactions. The skits not only pointed out things that were done incorrectly, but also illustrated a better way to handle situations. Over 220 Hillside employees and volunteers came to see *The Final Insult,* and the average number of patient complaints has dropped to about four per month. Perhaps even more to the point, now patients are offering praise to specific staff members and departments. This praise is beginning to outnumber the complaints.

One of Hillside's crowning achievements came almost as this book was going to press in the form of validation from the outside. The Joint Commission on Accreditation of Healthcare Organizations (JCAHO) is a private, not-for-profit organization that evaluates and accredits more than 8,000 health-care organizations, 5,300 of which are hospitals. In February 1996 JCAHO surveyed Hillside with extremely positive results. "Out of a possible 100 points, Hillside received a score of 93," said an elated Marijo Shuntich, BSN, Clinical Program Manager. "This is significantly above the average score of 88 for those hospitals and health-care organizations surveyed in 1995. It is also a vast improvement over our last score of 74."

Hillside's growth as a team-oriented institution able to focus on quality patient-care has been remarkable to see. Shuntich said because of their work on labor and management communication issues as well as their intensive work on developing a team-based culture, "we approached the survey preparation as we approach our day-to-day business—as a team where everyone has an equal voice."

Teamwork really does make a difference.

SIX

Coral Springs, Florida: "We Want to Be the Premier City in Florida to Live, Work, and Raise a Family"

Y ou might be hard pressed to find a more <u>un</u>likely place for self-directed teams than public service. The very structures of government employment seem to work for inertia and against change. Yet, the public sector monopoly is slowly being challenged by citizens tired of paying taxes and seeing city vehicles idling on the streets in the morning with three employees in the front seat reading the paper. And citizens are tired of calling to report a problem only to be put on hold, transferred, told to call another number at a different time, or any of many versions of the runaround. With union protection and an election every two years (or so), public service employees generally have secure jobs tucked within a system that is anathema to long-term accountability. Although individual public servants may have "customer delight" on the top of their agenda, little in most government work encourages, or even supports, such an attitude.

The very structures of government employment seem to work for inertia and against change.

Bunker mentality may best characterize the spirit of the public employee who daily faces demands from bosses, Jane O. and John Q. Public, with a supervisor whose best agenda may be to keep the waters tested for the latest change in temperature. Especially in the cases of large bureaucracies, the supervisor is least likely to be concerned with changes in the office that might run afoul of the agenda of an elected official with a single-year attention span. What a mess! On the other hand, what better place to have a smoothly running, efficient operation?

Some Background

Coral Springs, located 15 miles from Fort Lauderdale, is just over 30 years old (incorporated in 1963). It has a commission/city-manager form of government with four commissioners and a mayor all elected at large. The commission appoints a manager who is responsible for the overall operations of 15 departments. The population of Coral Springs is largely white (93 percent), one-third school-aged, and significantly family oriented. It has almost 31,000 households and a median income of $45,039, which puts Coral Springs at the top of the list for household income among major cities in the southeastern United States. The city employs 577 full and part-time employees whose business it is to

- Protect personal safety.
- Protect personal and public property.
- Provide athletic, recreational, and cultural services.
- Construct and maintain streets.
- Provide safe drinking water.
- Collect storm water.
- Treat and dispose of waste water.
- Maintain urban planning standards.
- Regulate building construction.
- Encourage commercial and industrial development.
- Manage the city's financial resources.
- Hire, develop, and administer benefit programs for employees.
- Provide information and data resources.
- Communicate information to the public.

While many employees of the city of Coral Springs had no doubt heard the word *empowerment* before, few realized just how important it would become to their lives and their livelihoods. In 1992 when the city commission hired Tony O'Rourke to be its new city manager, it signaled an honest to goodness paradigm shift for the employees and the residents of the city. The commissioners, all business people, thought the city could work better; they thought it could be more efficient, like a business. They hired Tony because he was of the same mind and came with a track record of helping other cities function more efficiently. The task ahead would be to change the structure of the city government and then change the mind-set of city employees. Figures 6–1 and 6–2 show the reality of Coral Springs when Tony arrived and his vision of how he would remake the city bureaucracy.

> *While many employees of the City of Coral Springs had no doubt heard the word empowerment before, few realized just how important it would become to their lives and their livelihoods.*

Tony's arrival signaled the birth of total quality management (TQM) for Coral Springs along with TQM's modus operandi—teams. For the new City Manager O'Rourke, and the four city commissioners, the change was a meeting of the minds—a convergence of two rivers, as one city employee put it. The city was going to run like a business and customer delight would be its product.

Figure 6–1 The City of Coral Springs Administration, June 1994

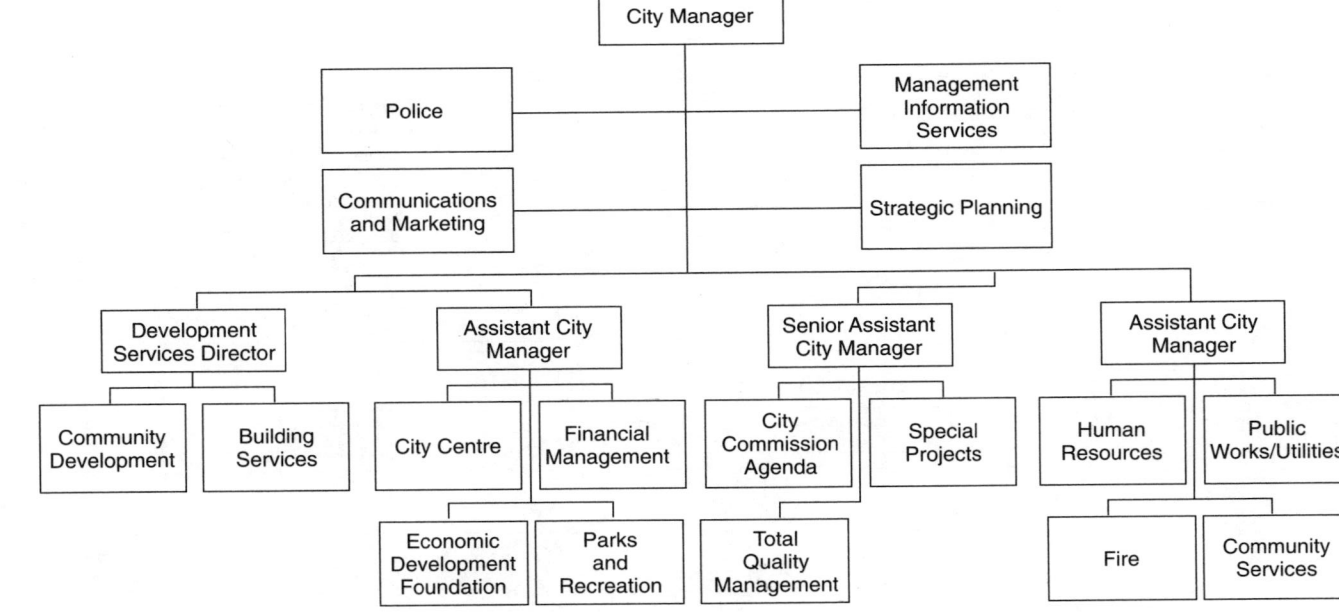

Figure 6–2   Tony O'Rourke's Vision

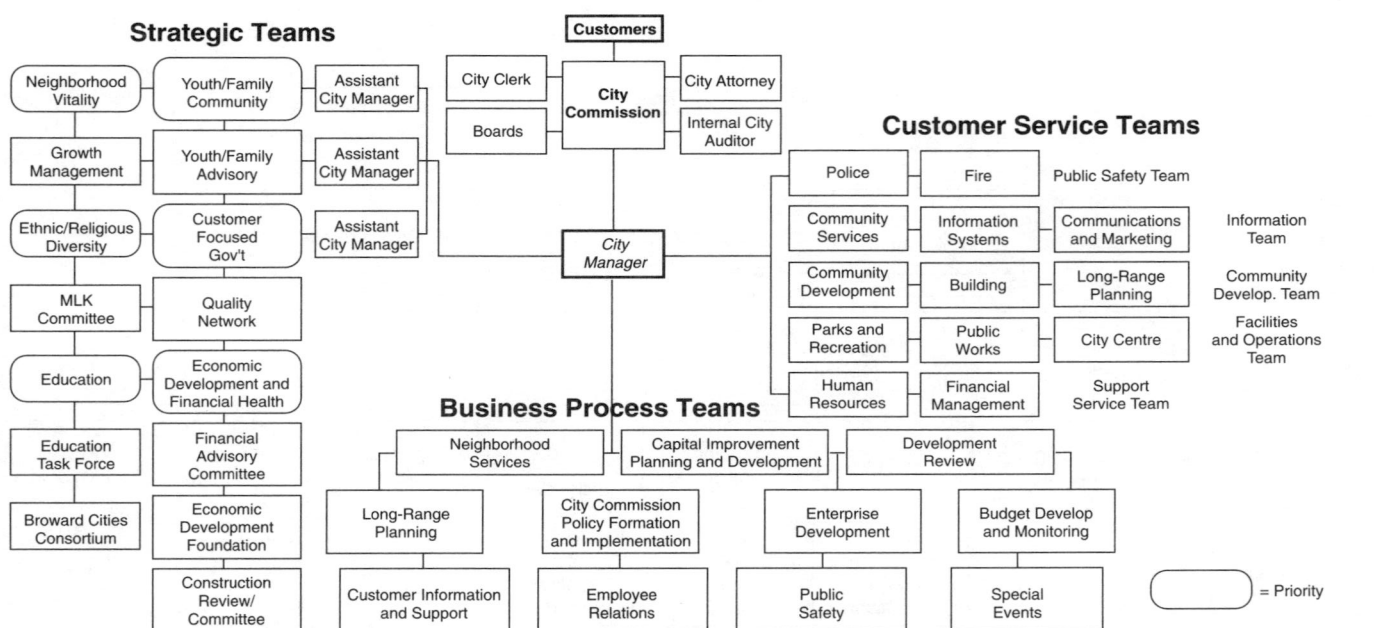

The Change Process

The city of Coral Springs has had an easier job than some organizations have had implementing teams—the city is relatively young, and therefore has less history to contend with, and the city commissioners are behind the program 100 percent. This means that resources are allocated, good team members are rewarded, and the goals are oriented to reflect the priorities established by the city commission. In other words, a refreshing sense of purpose and direction permeates the work of the government of Coral Springs, Florida.

There were resisters, however. Many of the directors had worked for the city for 20 years or more; they had seen managers come and managers go. They knew programs didn't have to interfere with the way they wanted to do business. They and some of their staff made up the Toxic Twenty you'll find in every change effort. There were plenty of employees who said things like, "I don't want to work this hard." "A city isn't a business—we're working too hard." Tony, though, had experience with just these kinds of people and he knew to focus on those who wanted to make things work, not on those who didn't. Some people were given incentives to find employment elsewhere, some were transferred, and some changed their minds about the program and came on board.

The resistant employees had company among many in the local media. Newspaper editorials ran angry columns deriding the ambitions of the city commissioners to make city government more efficient. In particular the newspaper editorials attacked the city's allocation of resources (money) for training and development of city employees. These attacks abated once city residents felt the improvements. There is, after all, nothing like success to justify change.

Figure 6–3   Information cycles from team to team for greater efficiency

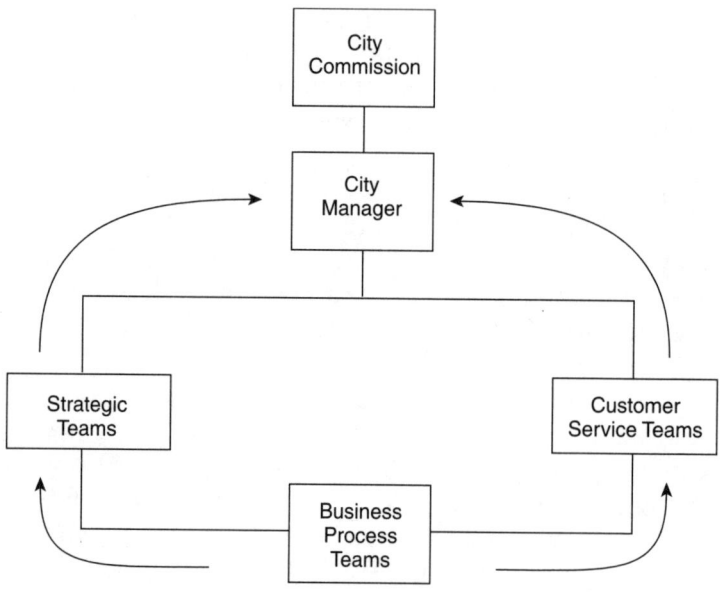

The New Government Organization

Tony implemented tiers of teams—strategic, business process, and customer service, as shown in Figure 6–2. As Figure 6–3 shows, each team cycles information into the others and is, in turn, affected by the information it receives. The commission writes the mission of the city (as quoted in the title of this chapter) and identifies strategic priorities for the city to achieve that will fulfill the mission goal. There are six strategic priorities:

1. Customer focused government.
2. Excellence in education.
3. Neighborhood vitality.
4. Youth, family, and community.
5. Financial health and economic development.
6. Respect for ethnic and religious diversity.

These priorities provide philosophical and political direction to the city and a direction for allocating resources. They are set for at least five years. Annual goals and measures are specified in an annual strategic plan. From this plan, operating departments derive a road map that they supplement with lists of tasks that will result in a detailed work order. City teams use four requirements to determine the quality of their work:

1. Does the service or program reduce the cycle time for delivering services and programs?
2. Does it increase customers' access to city services and programs?
3. Does it reduce the cost customers have to pay through taxes or users' fees for city services and programs?
4. Does it provide services and programs at service levels that meet customer expectations?

The city mission statement means that customer satisfaction has the highest priority, and that satisfaction is measured not only in services rendered, but also in the way the city manages all of the resources for which it is responsible—to be blunt, how well the city spends its residents' money. When the city thinks it can do better with a specific service, it takes a hard look at the problem, and as a result may bid the work out. That's what happened to the city garage employees just one short year after the teams and TQM were initiated.

> *The city mission statement means that customer satisfaction has the highest priority, and that satisfaction is measured not only in services rendered, but also in the way the city manages all of the resources for which it is responsible—to be blunt, how well the city spends its residents' money.*

The City Garage—One Motivated Team

In June 1993 the city commission voted to seek bids for vehicle maintenance in an attempt to cut the city's budget and improve service. The city services monopoly was being challenged—it came as a shock to the city garage who was just forming its pilot team project. With an effort that surprised many in its intensity and professionalism, the equipment division of the city garage cranked into overdrive to, in effect, bid for their own jobs. In a sometimes painful process, the fleet maintenance crew formed a committee and reviewed how the division operated. For four months, workers covered for the committee members who worked late and on Saturdays to research and write the proposal. Said one mechanic-committee member of the process, "I never knew how much it cost them to run the garage." The team made a videotape to illustrate their commitment to quality service and supplemented their presentation with testimonials from satisfied customers—fellow city employees of the police, fire, and parks and recreation departments. Working as a team, they looked at the tasks that were the city garage's responsibility, as well as the budget that the commission wanted cut. Their proposal, pitted against bids from the private sector, was successful: The mechanics team brought their budget down, from $1 million to $750,000, (and within $25,000 of the best private bid) by eliminating three positions from the garage. One employee retired, and two transferred to other departments in the city. Figure 6–4 is the city garage team's own summary of their successful process.

Working together to prepare a successful bid was a great bonding mechanism, to say the least. The city garage crew felt like a family after their endeavor; they were well on their way to being a team. According to the supervisor, it took about a month after defeating Ryder in the bid process for a second phase of team growth to set in. Team members became confused about just what decisions they could make, should make, or wanted to make as a team, and what decisions should be left to the supervisor. It was the supervisor's job to listen to his crew sound off and then to send them out to do what they thought best. After some time, the crew learned that their supervisor would stand behind their decisions, and most of the mechanics were better able to act out of the authority

Figure 6–4 The City Garage Team's Journey

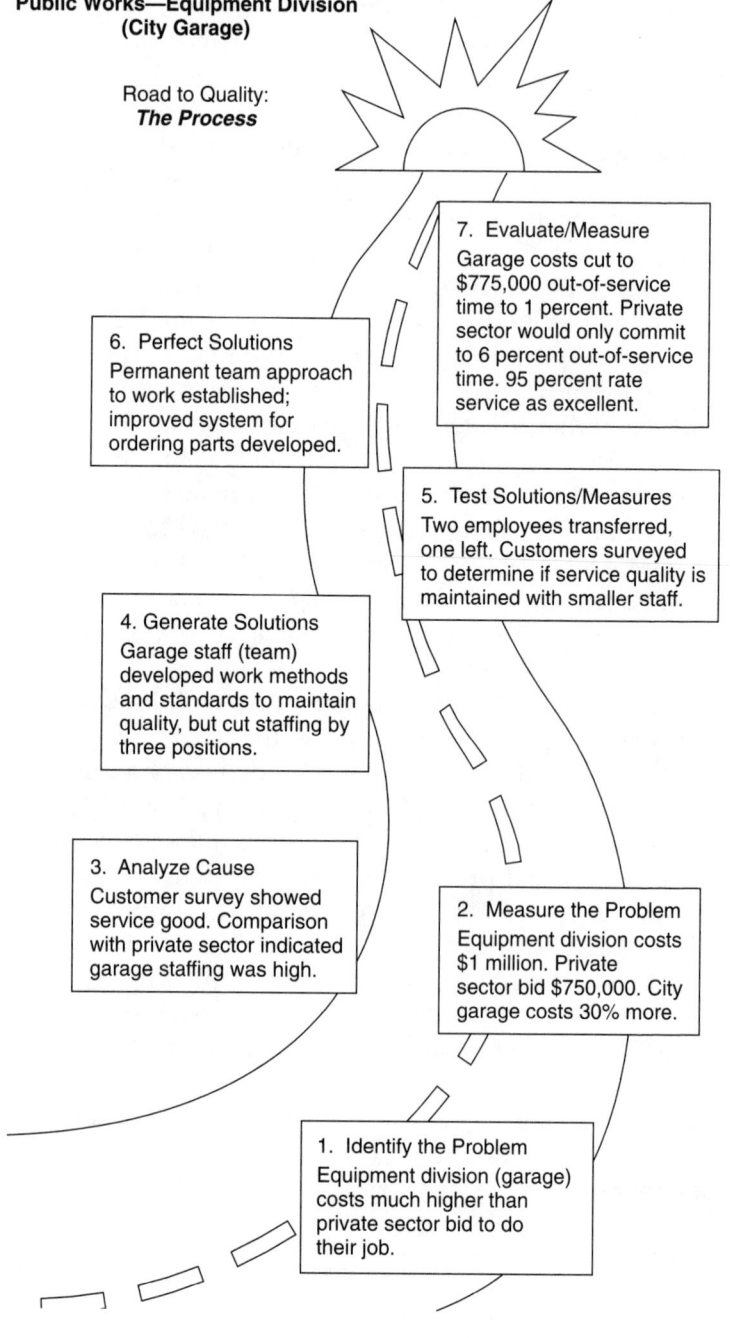

Public Works—Equipment Division (City Garage)

Road to Quality:
The Process

7. Evaluate/Measure
Garage costs cut to $775,000 out-of-service time to 1 percent. Private sector would only commit to 6 percent out-of-service time. 95 percent rate service as excellent.

6. Perfect Solutions
Permanent team approach to work established; improved system for ordering parts developed.

5. Test Solutions/Measures
Two employees transferred, one left. Customers surveyed to determine if service quality is maintained with smaller staff.

4. Generate Solutions
Garage staff (team) developed work methods and standards to maintain quality, but cut staffing by three positions.

3. Analyze Cause
Customer survey showed service good. Comparison with private sector indicated garage staffing was high.

2. Measure the Problem
Equipment division costs $1 million. Private sector bid $750,000. City garage costs 30% more.

1. Identify the Problem
Equipment division (garage) costs much higher than private sector bid to do their job.

they had. One mechanic maintained a "CYA" attitude; he had been burned by previous management and found it hard to take responsibility for making his own decisions. The team and the supervisor were able to help him see his behavior through training videos that showed others similarly in need of attitude adjustments.

As the team progressed, so did their changes. They dispensed with lead mechanics, assuming that responsibility themselves. They devised their own schedules for repairs and

> *As the team progressed, so did their changes.*

preventive maintenance using four chalkboards to track the work. One board tracks all preventive maintenance and when vehicles were last serviced. A second board lists work that has come in to be done and allows mechanics to take jobs in order of priority. A third board lists all mechanics and major areas of repair. When a mechanic takes a job he or she notes it on the board so that customers can tell if their vehicle is being worked on and by whom. The fourth board lists completed work so that the administrative assistant can answer calls from customers about the status of their units.

The city garage handles about 1,100 service orders a month, mostly for the city's 530 vehicles. But the mechanics can work on anything with a motor, noted the supervisor, who adds that he is happily working as a facilitator not a dictator. Some of the other accomplishments of the garage team include

- Taking over maintenance of 19 vehicles leased to the building department because the leasing company service was slow and inadequate.

- Converting several police cars and city trucks to propane gas and reconditioning equipment whenever possible.
- Purchasing the tool needed to repair hydraulic hoses instead of paying to replace worn-out hoses.
- Contracting with other towns to do specific maintenance work (i.e., maintaining Parkland's fire trucks), thus earning money for the city of Coral Springs.

The experience brought notice from the public, editorials of praise in the newspapers, and apparently a sustained spike in job satisfaction for the team members of the city garage.

Tony O'Rourke faced impediments from the public, the press, and his own staff. The press howled about the special requirements of TQM, the money spent on meetings, training, reports, and the language (TQM-speak), which can be a lot to buy into, especially if you are cynical. The 20–60–20 curve prevailed in the departments of Coral Springs, as it does elsewhere. Tony had to prove himself as sincere, had to show his workers that they would not be penalized for trying, and had to help those who would not try, to find the exit door. Since it is very difficult to fire government employees, Tony used incentives like early retirement and other buyouts. He had to train his senior staff and he had to communicate the change to all the employees of the city of Coral Springs so everyone knew the same thing and knew what it meant. Tony explained:

> Using teams to become "better, faster, and cheaper" than the competition is a difficult, time-consuming, stressful, and risky undertaking for any traditional organization." In each of several

ways, the organization must make much more than a slight change of course. It must alter its course, in essence, by a full 180 degrees. Moving from internally driven to customer driven is a 180-degree change of course for the organization. Moving from functionally focused to process focused is a 180-degree change. Moving from management centered to employee involved is also a 180-degree change of course. These shifts represent and require a major organizational paradigm change.

Not all the departments in Coral Springs were successful, or even interested in competing with private interests for their jobs. For instance, the city centre program (the arts program) was privatized once the commission determined that Coral Springs residents would be better served by another vendor at a total loss of two jobs, the director and assistant director. The other employees were absorbed into other areas of city employment.

Quality Is Never Done

The work is not complete. The city must keep improving to continue delivering "customer delight." Here's a partial to-do list:

1. Management teams should be designed and staffed in a single process, instead of vertical functions; departments should organize around processes *not* functions.
2. A greater awareness of the interdependence of organizational components should be fostered.
3. The principle challenge is to improve upon cross-functional *processes*.

4. Departmental (functions) should be grouped and consolidated to facilitate necessary interdepartmental communication. For example, public works could be combined with parks and recreation; public safety with code enforcement.
5. Streamlining the organizational structure should be accomplished through team management on a project-by-project basis.

One of Tony O'Rourke's reorganization principles to make an organization more responsive to its customers is to involve and empower employees and teams. Most organizations, which are internally driven (as opposed to customer focused) and functionally focused (as opposed to cross-functional), are also management centered. In other words, managers see themselves as the central players in the organization and assume they need to control almost everything. As a result, managers (often inadvertently) can deny employees the information, skills, experience, and authority that employees must have in order to make meaningful improvements in their own areas.

> *Managers (often inadvertently) can deny employees the information, skills, experience, and authority that employees must have in order to make meaningful improvements in their own areas.*

In contrast, notes O'Rourke, successfully changing organizations recognizes that the world is moving too quickly for managers to

Know enough. . .
Fast enough. . .
About enough things. . .
To be right enough. . .
Enough of the time. . .
To control enough things correctly. . .
To keep the enterprise from being swamped. . .

What's the alternative to "management-centeredness"? It's *employee involvement.* Employee involvement and empowerment make up the systematic effort to build and benefit from the knowledge, skills, and commitment of the workforce. By their closeness to work processes and to the customer—and by their sheer numbers—employees can know enough fast enough to improve things on a grand scale. The people who work closest to the problem know the most about how to solve the problem.

> *What's the alternative to "management-centeredness"? It's employee involvement.*

At Coral Springs, employee involvement is not an end in itself. It's just the best means to increase customer satisfaction, and reduce cycle times and costs at the same time. Because of the enormous resources it brings to bear on the problem, employee involvement is the activating mechanism for all three kinds of improvement. That's why few organizations have sustained major improvements in costs, cycle times, and customer satisfaction without a major increase in employee involvement.

SEVEN

Team Tools for Development and Delight

This is our learning-by-doing chapter—when it comes to teams that is the most valuable experience to have. In teamwork, after all, the emphasis is on the work, on the progress toward goals, on movement. In this chapter, I have outlined several exercises we used during our training that are designed to be both fun and instructive.

Activity 1:
Just before the Tropical Island Experience

There are two parts to this assignment: the first is an individual work assignment, the second is the teamwork. You are allowed 10 minutes for the first part and 20 minutes for the second.

The Situation A small touring boat has been severely damaged by a tropical storm. The boat has been carried miles and miles off course into uncharted, shark-infested waters. The boat cannot be repaired. It will sink in 30 minutes.

There are 10 passengers aboard this sinking ship and only one lifeboat, a rowboat. The lifeboat can only carry seven people. The nearest land is an island 15 nautical miles away. The island is uninhabited and tropical. By the lifeboat, the journey is about two hours or more.

The seven passengers you select for the lifeboat have two goals, one short-term, one long-term:

Short-Term Goal:	Row two hours to get to the island safely. Of the two hours one will be at night where the island disappears from sight.
Long-Term Goal:	Once the passengers arrive on the island they will be stranded forever. They must set up a new society that can be self-managing and self-perpetuating.

Individual Assignments First Task: Each team member must rank order the passengers from 1 to 10. The first seven will go on the lifeboat, the remaining three passengers will be left behind.

Every passenger must be assigned a number. The passengers who are ranked 8, 9, and 10 *must* be left on the ship that is sinking in the SHARK-INFESTED WATERS.

Second Task: Once you have ranked your passengers from 1 to 10, you then must select the following from among the seven who will go on the lifeboat:

1. A captain/leader.
2. First officer/vice president.
3. Team counselor/mediator.

These three passengers will make up the leadership team; your choices are critical to the survival of your entire team.

Third Task: Once you decide who stays on the sinking boat in shark-infested waters and who goes on the lifeboat to the deserted desert island, you then must write a paragraph explaining your reasons for choosing the three individuals to be left behind. Be able to strongly defend your positions.

Team Activity

(Teams should range between 6 and 15 members only.) Each team member brings to the group his or her individual ranking of the passengers, a list of the team leaders for the lifeboat crew, and a defense of those choices. The team must arrive at one list and one set of leaders, and achieve consensus on its reasons for its choices. The group must also agree on the reasons for leaving three passengers on the sinking ship in the shark-infested waters. The team has 20 minutes to reach consensus.

The Passenger List

Age	The Passengers
40	Female—African American Catholic nun who is a clergy professional.
65	Male—white, farmer from Iowa.
29	Female—Asian American, microbiologist who was blind from birth.
21	Male—white, college football lineman.
54	Male—white, police officer with a loaded gun, from the Bronx in New York City. The gun has only two bullets.
38	Female—white, airline pilot for a major U. S. airline company.
32	Male—African American stowaway who is a member of Mensa. An absolute genius. Also homeless by choice and antisocial. Does not like or trust people. Stowed away to get away from society. PhD in Mechanical Engineering.
48	Male—corporate executive for a Fortune 500 corporation who is a Hispanic American.
35	Female—African-American, the corporate executive's wife who is seven months pregnant with their first child.

44   Male—white, general practitioner M.D. who is chief of staff for a major hospital and HIV positive.

Evaluating the Activity

Time is up. How did you do? Did you conclude that some of the people were worth more than others and construct a win-lose situation? Did you, perhaps, realize that you were constructing two teams, each with a chance at survival, and construct a win-win scenario? Granted, there was not enough information for a totally informed and logical decision on whom to leave behind and whom to select for the lifeboat. That in fact is usually the case, and we all have to make decisions with the facts at hand. We have to interpret those facts to determine their relative value and significance. In fact, this exercise even includes extraneous information, stuff that has nothing to do with an informed and logical decision, but that probably weighs heavily in a person's values. The weight we put on the various kinds of information available for consideration is usually value driven. In this exercise, each participant got to experience their values firsthand as he or she sifted through the personnel information and made the selection of crew for the lifeboat.

One of the challenges for building a team out of a diverse workforce is that each team member brings his or her values, morals, beliefs, and traditions to the team. Sometimes, these personal and cultural slants are unconscious—they may never have been examined. These are some of our most strongly held beliefs and values and they are tied to our emotions. An unexamined, emotional stance interferes with our ability to look at situations objectively and consider different opinions. Without this ability, team consensus may never happen. Most self-managing teams must be able to make critical decisions on a consensual basis. So, an ability to know thyself is a valuable team skill.

Consider the following questions as you and your team discuss the exercise:

- What were the major obstacles to consensus and how were they overcome by the team?
- How long did it take the team to reach a total agreement?
- What decision-making process did the team use to reach consensus?
- If you are doing this exercise with more than one team, have each team share their rank order and explain the reason for the ranking.

If you approach the problem from a win-win point of view, then you can choose the three travelers with the best opportunity to survive in the sinking boat. See Appendix A for the correct passenger list. The mechanical engineer is a genius and may have the best possible chance to arrive at a mechanical solution to keep the boat afloat; the police officer has two bullets, which ought to dissuade a shark or two; and the medical doctor will further the survival odds with his knowledge of first aid. In addition, each of these individuals has faced life and death situations on a daily basis and achieved peak performance under peak pressure.

In the lifeboat we put the airline pilot who has certain navigational skills, and we make her captain because we recognize that she already is comfortable leading a crew based on her experience as a pilot. We make the corporate executive who is skilled at administration and leadership (by virtue of his rank in a Fortune 500 company) the first officer, and the Catholic nun who is a clergy professional the team counselor because of her skills with mediation. The college football lineman, a team player, ought to be strong enough for the rowing that's ahead; the microbiologist and the farmer should have good survival skills for cultivating and other life-skills on the island; and the corporate executive's wife is clearly fertile.

If you are saying I have made assumptions also, you are correct. However, my assumptions were based on the skill sets of the individuals as reflected by their titles; I was not distracted by race, sex, or age. My direction was also firmly toward win-win and that is a much stronger position in a group decision-making process than win-lose.

Team Decision Making

There are primarily three different kinds of decision-making processes, consensual, democratic, and unilateral (or autocratic). Each has its place in your team's daily work and it is important to know when one is more appropriate than another and how to participate in each process.

Consensual Decision Making

Reaching consensus as a team means presenting a unified front. If my team has decided that next month's public relations campaign will feature conservative leaders in my company, then that becomes my decision also. It would be disloyal and disruptive for me to go to the vice president and say that I really wanted to see Hank featured, but *they* said he was too liberal for the campaign. A consensus-based decision means that every team member has 70 percent buy-in. It does not require that each member love the decision, but we can assume that every team member can live with it and own it as their team's decision. Reaching consensus is a we versus I situation in which insisting on an individual opinion would show a lack of support for the team. Consensus-based decisions can only be truly arrived at in a win-win environment. They require and reflect respect for other team members' points of view and concerns. These decisions are not easily arrived at, and in fact, when a consensus is needed and cannot be found, the team should see that they are not ready to reach consensus. Put the matter on the shelf for a designated period of time and let team members think about it. After a little stewing, the juices will have tenderized the issue and consensus may be possible.

What kinds of decisions are best handled by consensus?

First, these are the really important direction-finding decisions that matter for at least two reasons: they have extrinsic importance to the success of the company because these decisions are at the heart of the team's scope of work, and they have intrinsic importance in that they show how well the team can work. Reaching consensus on a difficult issue is, as you have experienced, hard to do. Second, these are the decisions that require reflection and benefit from discussion. These are the kinds of decisions that only teams can make, and teams tend to make better decisions than individuals. The whole is greater than the sum of its parts, after all. Depending on your team's scope of work and charter, consensus may be required as you consider terminating a team member, budget priorities, strategic planning, goal setting, and hiring or selecting new team members.

Unilateral Decision Making

There comes a time when there is no time for discussion. In a crisis, a team must be able to decide a course of action and, as the captain says, "make it so." These decisions are made by the team leader or the coach, the captain of your ship. They are made with the fullest consideration of the team's charter so that the actions further the team's direction and do not send it off into left field.

What kinds of decisions are best handled unilaterally?

- A team member quits in the middle of a campaign and needs to be replaced in a matter of days.
- The supply source for a manufacturing run is cut off because of a strike in the transportation sector.
- A customer calls angry about the way his account is being serviced and threatens to take his business elsewhere.

Each of the above examples is a crisis that threatens to disrupt business severely. In each case, the team leader or coach would be actually remiss if she did not respond to and/or rectify the problem. Yes, the team needs to be informed of the crisis and the response, and it needs an opportunity to discuss the decision. There may be important lessons, for instance, in the sudden resignation of an important team member or in an angry customer. Unilateral decisions are not an excuse for not talking. They are decisions made swiftly to solve a crisis. The team will back the decision through the crisis (in all but the most incredible circumstances) and then reinvolve itself in the decision in a debriefing session at the earliest opportunity. This is not to second-guess the team leader, but to understand what happened and what can be learned from the situation that will be useful in the future.

Majority Rule

Not every decision requires the unity of a consensus or the quick thinking of a team leader. Sometimes it's okay to have winners and losers. Knowing when it's okay to win some and lose some and when everyone has to feel mostly okay about a decision can be tricky, especially with a newly formed team. Generally, though, operational decisions that are timely in nature and have deadlines attached are appropriate for team votes.

The fact that majority rules, however, does not mean that the majority is smarter. There is nothing in a democracy that suggests it is okay to disrespect another's opinion, thoughts, or stance. And there can be little more divisive than a smug winner because a decision went his or her way. There is absolutely no room for that kind of behavior on a team. The voting process should be viewed as a means to an end. The decisions that are made by team vote should be recurring decisions, and should come after a discussion to consider the pros and cons of one action over another.

What kinds of decisions are best made by majority rule?

- Vacation scheduling or holiday work schedules.
- Customer service decisions.
- Customer site-visit schedules.

In short, majority rule works in either/or situations following a discussion that lays out any consequences of a particular option. The decision is for one option over another, and not one team member over another. If personalities are getting in the way, it's time to talk to your coach.

Activity 2: Collaboration Can Be Fun

Being on a team can result in some of the most creative experiences of your professional life. It can truly be said that teams have more fun. They do work hard, though, to be productive and they always follow the rules of the road—once they have made them.

Risk Taking Divide your group into teams of six or more members.

1. The team must develop seven ground rules on how they conduct themselves as they work together. They will need to write their ground rules on a flip chart and post them where they can be accessed readily.
2. The team must develop a marketing plan to sell a newly created product for consumers.
   - They must give the product an interesting and catchy name.
   - They must develop a creative slogan around their product line.
   - They must develop a creative logo to represent their product.
   - And finally, they must develop a two-minute commercial jingle that all team members will sing together. The team can borrow the tune, but the lyrics must be their own.

Teams have 60 minutes for the ground rules and 90 minutes for the project. At the end, each team will present and perform its commercials. A judge, sufficiently objective and incorruptible, should award gold, silver, and bronze medals.

Evaluating the Activity

How long did it take your team to come up with seven operating rules? Did you think the rules should be situation specific, such as sterilization procedures for proper operating room hygiene? If so, then you were handicapped by not knowing the task at hand. There are, however, genuine rules of conduct that support teamwork in any situation and that provide guidelines for conducting business:

- Listen to your team members.
- Respect ideas that are different from your own.
- Don't interrupt.
- No sarcasm.
- Agree on a decision-making process (consensual, democratic, or unilateral).
- Stick to the task at hand.
- Analyze the idea, not the person.

The seven guidelines above can be used in almost any team situation to further progress toward any goal. Remember, it takes teamwork to accomplish a team's work. Make certain that your team members are facilitating the team, and not the individual, effort.

What decision-making process did you find yourselves using to meet your goal? There were a lot of decisions to be made:

- Establish ground rules.
- Choose a product and name it.

- Develop a marketing campaign that includes a slogan, logo, and jingle.

There was very little time in which to make them. I hope you didn't resort to passive unilateralism where the most energetic member of your group took over and did all your work for you. It's very unlikely your group had time to reach consensus on all the decisions that needed to be made. Most likely, the most efficient procedure would be majority rules. Given the ground rules calling for attentive listening and respect, the majority rules procedure would probably work the best and still maintain team spirit.

Activity 3: The Blind Leading the Blind

All things being equal, we are probably more often in a situation of the blind leading the blind than we would like to acknowledge. It is truly rare that a leader actually can see ahead to determine what is coming. Most often decisions are made based on experience, hunches, data, and other stuff—not on omniscience. So, the following is an exercise in reality.

Materials Needed:
Rope, about 20 feet long, for each team.
Blindfolds for each team member.
A parking-lot–sized space to move about.

Instructions: Team should have no fewer than 6 and no more than 12 members each. Have the team members stand in a straight line, facing you, the trainer or exercise leader.

Have team members put on their blindfolds so that they cannot see around them. (No cheating!)

Place the rope at the feet of the team members and have the team members bend down and grab the rope with both hands. They are to hold the rope with both hands at all times.

Assignment: While holding onto the rope with both hands and blindfolded, team members must arrange themselves to create a square. Once they think the task is accomplished, they must place the rope at their feet, step away and take off their blindfolds to survey their work.

Team members put their blindfolds back on and pick up the rope (in whatever geometric shape it appears) and form a single file line. The team leader, who is not wearing a blindfold, must lead his team into the classroom without touching the rope or any other team member.

Evaluating the Activity

It is very difficult to be on a team when no one knows what they are doing, and there is nothing like putting everyone at sixes and sevens to find that out. The chaos that ensues when a team of professionals, grasping a rope with both hands, tries to form a square while blindfolded will not abate until the team members learn to listen to one other, find a leader, and follow that leader and his or her idea to its fruition. Because the situation resembles a crisis, this is no time for democratic or consensual decision making.

This is an exercise in the development of trust through risk taking. It is also an appropriate time for unilateral decision making—the first task approximates a crisis by suddenly and arbitrarily denying team members essential sensory information with which to complete a task. The only real consensual decision is choosing a leader; after that it behooves each member to listen and follow orders! If you are surprised, check out the discussion on decision making earlier in this chapter.

Those who participated in the exercise should debrief with a discussion of the following questions:

1. How did your square turn out?
2. What were the major obstacles in performing the task?
3. What strategy did your team use to accomplish the task?
4. How did you feel walking blindfolded while holding onto the rope?
5. What do you think the rope represents?

Activity 4: Brainstorming for Teams

Brainstorming can be a very fruitful process for finding your way out of the desert before you turn into dust. It can also get your team out of idea gridlock—when nothing you have tried seems right. But, to work brainstorming requires solid team relationships because it requires trust. Nothing shuts down a brainstorming session more quickly than the words, or the look, that says, "what a stupid idea that is." In fact, a few dumb ideas may have to tumble out before the idea that the team can build on falls to the table. And in brainstorming, the process really is one where ideas fall out—if someone is being cautious, or editing their thoughts, then they aren't brainstorming. This is also why it is so important to have deeply held respect for team members—when things are falling out it is easy to let slip some very personal responses.

In the following activities, if multiple teams are participating you can have a competition to see which team gets the correct answer first. Remember, try to avoid a competition within teams—brainstorming is a synergistic activity in which team members build on each other's activity, not a competitive activity. The answers to exercises 1 through 7 will be found in Appendix A.

1.

$$\textbf{000}$$
$$\textbf{000}$$
$$\textbf{000}$$

In three straight lines, without lifting your pen from the paper, connect all nine circles.

2.

$$\textbf{000}$$
$$\textbf{000}$$
$$\textbf{000}$$

Using four straight lines, without lifting your pen from the paper, connect all nine circles.

3.

$$\underline{\textbf{iii}}$$
$$\textbf{0000}$$
$$\textbf{000}$$
$$\textbf{00}$$
$$\textbf{0}$$

Decode this puzzle—what well known phrase is being symbolized here?

4.

$$\frac{0}{\text{Ph.D., MD}}$$

Decode and write out the message.

5.

<u>Knee</u>
Light

Decode and find two phrases.

6.

Ecnalg

Decode and write the phrase.

7.

Decode and write the phrase.

Activity 5: Careful Listening, Better Hearing

The following is a listening test. What it tests is not actual hearing acuity, but the ability to listen to what is really being said. You may find that what you think you hear and what is being said are two different things.

Read the following questions to your team, and have them write down what they believe are the correct answers. You can only read the questions once. The correct answers will be found in Appendix A.

1. A man builds an ordinary house with four sides. Each side has a southern exposure. A bear comes to the door and rings the doorbell. What color is the bear?

2. You are in a dark, damp cave with only one match. You have a kerosene lamp, an oil lantern, and a wood burning stove. Which do you light first to obtain maximum heat?

3. How many animals of each species did Moses take aboard the ark before the great flood?

4. Is there any federal law against a man marrying his widow's sister?

5. An archeologist claims that he's dug up a coin that is clearly dated 46 B.C. Why is this person not telling the truth?

6. Is there a Fourth of July over in England?

7. A feathered vertebrate enclosed in the grasping organ has an estimated worth higher than duo encapsulated in the branch shrub. What does this really mean?

Evaluating the Activity

There are so many things that interfere with how well we listen. The most common barrier, perhaps, is simply having an interior monologue that blocks our attention. This usually means we are distracted when we need to be paying attention, and we aren't listening. The best way to handle this problem, I have found, is first to recognize the jabbering interior voice. Then, instead of squelching it (which usually doesn't work) pay attention to what seems to be the problem.

- It may be physical discomfort: cold feet, headache, stomach ache, and the like. These are signs that should not be ignored. Take a break, tell your teammates you need to take care of whatever is the problem, and then come back. You will be much better able to listen, I guarantee it.
- You may be distracted by something that happened earlier in the day. Tell yourself that you will definitely find time to think about the boss' reaction to your progress report, or whatever seems to have caught your attention, later, but right now you have to pay attention to the team discussion.
- You may be distracted by something that will be happening in the future. How often have I sat so absorbed by my forthcoming presentation that I missed every other word of what was being said! This can be helped by preparing rigorously and then reassuring yourself that you've done the best you can, now you have to listen to the discussion at hand.

Some people listen very intently, but still don't listen well. Did you, for instance "hear" the leader say Noah instead of Moses on the third question? If so, you were inferring Noah because that was what you expected to hear. Inferences can cause lots of problems when the subject is counterintuitive or otherwise complex. A second bad habit is jumping to conclusions—that is leaping to a decision instead of thinking. Did you say that only America could have a Fourth of July? Well, there is a fourth of July on every July calendar.

To develop your listening ability practice two skills: (1) learn to reflect, or mirror what is being said, and (2) write it down. Reflecting requires a passive receptivity—you aren't tense with preconceived notions about what will be said. You are able to take the information and almost make a picture. This is especially helpful in deductive reasoning situations like that posed in the first question in the exercise. If you can take in what is being said and picture it, then you can probably understand it. Taking notes can be a useful tool for keeping track of complex information. If you were taking notes during the last question you may have deciphered the complexities as you went along.

Activity 6: Talk to People (TTP)

In all my workshops over the years, I've gotten to know a lot of people. This list of characteristics comes from all that experience. If you are working with groups of at least 20 people, I'm certain someone owns a Longaberger basket.

Instructions: Talk to people in this room and find out who matches these descriptions. Once you find a match get their signature on the appropriate line. Each line must have a different person, no twofers allowed. The first paper with all blanks filled in gets a prize.

Find A Person Who:

1. Cannot swim _____

2. Shares the same birth month as yourself

     _____

3. Sings in the choir _____

4. Plays the piano _____

5. Owns a Longaberger _____

6. Never owned a dog as a pet _____

7. Owns a cat as a pet _____

8. Was raised on a farm _____

9. Is a grandparent _____

10. Served in armed forces _____

11. Has red hair _____

12. Has never been to NYC _____

13. Has been on television _____

14. Attended a Big 10 university _____

15. Is the oldest sibling in the family _____

16. Had major surgery _____

17. Is afraid of heights _____

18. Has never flown in a plane _____

19. Has been to Jamaica _____

20. Has met a U.S. President _____

Evaluating The Activity

Did anyone suggest doing this with a team effort?
How was that suggestion received? In a team effort,
the task can be completed in about five minutes.
Individually, completing the list requires much more
time, energy, and hassle. But, probably what happened
was your group turned the activity into an individual
competition and worked against each other. I've been
in groups where the person who suggested a team

effort is almost booed off the floor. We have a long way to go in undoing the narcissistic, individualistic inclination of our culture. And, getting there will be a lot of work—it takes much learning for working together to become as natural an inclination as working against each other has become. But once we are out there working together it will be a different world we live in, one with more accomplishment, and more strength than we've ever had in our fortresses of one.

POSTSCRIPT

Lessons from the Chinese Bamboo Tree

One theme of this book has been that implementing high-performance teams is more of a continuous process than a single project and that teams are more like organisms than they are like organizations. Teams are not a cure-all for all the problems facing a company, a church, a hospital, or a city. Teams are a tool to be used appropriately, skillfully, and patiently for them to be effective.

Teams are similar to computers—just having one does not guarantee increased production or efficiency—without the proper installation, without timely training, and without effective application both will cause more problems than they will ever solve.

I would like to close this book on teams with a word on one of the most critical elements in this entire team development process, the word is time. My friends, building a successful team takes so much time. There is the up-front investment of planning, preparation, and site visits which can take about 6–9 months, the pilot project phases which can take another 12 months, and the continuous time spent training: unlearning, learning, and relearning critical skills in order to be successful. Finally you have to endure the five stages of team maturation for another 3–5 years.

Many people celebrate the General Motors Saturn plant's team culture. People rave about their cute cars with the great sales process called the "No Dicker Sticker®." Few people realize that it took the Saturn Corporation eight long arduous years to make a profit, while using self-managing teams. This company had all the advantages of a brand new plant built from scratch, modern equipment, major capital investments from its parent company, tremendous commitment to training, collaborative relationship with the UAW, which supported the team culture and an intense marketing campaign. And yet with all of these built-in advantages their plant struggled to profitability—WHY? Major change takes time.

Making teams work is a lot like trying to grow the most difficult tree in the world, the Chinese bamboo tree. A farmer takes a seed and plants it in the soil and waters the soil, fertilizes the soil, and weeds the soil every day for a full year. After a full year of this daily routine the farmer looks out to survey his handiwork and sees nothing but what he had when he first started, flat land with no sprouts, no signs of life, nothing. Years two, three, and four are the exact same way. Can you possibly imagine working a total of 1,460 consecutive days and seeing nothing for your labor?

What emotions are generated from such unrewarded commitment? Frustration, anger, disappointment, apathy? Investing in a major change process like self-managing teams can make you feel the same way. You have invested years of time in the consideration process, the design process, the training process, the pilot process and people are still complaining, still griping; the same problems have not been completely resolved and you wonder whose idea was this team thing in the first place. Let's go back to our example of the Chinese bamboo tree.

After four years, no growth is seen, so what keeps this farmer motivated to continue his work? The farmer clearly and fully understands the growing processes of this tree. To the untrained eye he seems to be a fool, but the farmer knows that he will have to get to the third month of the fifth year when this seemingly dormant seed grows into a tree that is ninety feet tall. Four years nothing, three months 90 feet.

The question becomes did this tree grow ninety feet in three months or did it grow 90 feet in five years? The answer is clearly five years. During the first four years when nothing seems to be occurring on the surface, the farmer knows that the seed is growing underground. It is growing a deep root system that will be able to support a tree that will grow 90 feet in 3 months.

May all your team endeavors bear such well-supported fruit.

APPENDIX A

Here are the answers to the puzzles from Chapter 7.

Activity #1 Just before The Tropical Island Experience

There is a correct answer to this puzzle, that is the one which divides the passengers into teams based on giving each team its best chance at survival—win-win.

Age	The Passengers

<u>Lifeboat Crew</u>

38	Female—white, airline pilot for a major U.S. airline company. (captain)
48	Male—corporate executive for a Fortune 500 corporation who is a Hispanic American. (first officer)
40	Female—African American Catholic nun who is a clergy professional (counselor)
21	Male—white, college football lineman.
29	Female—Asian American, microbiologist who was blind from birth.
65	Male—white, farmer from Iowa.
35	The corporate executive's wife who is African American and seven months pregnant with their first child.

54   Male—white, police officer with a
            loaded gun, from the Bronx in New
            York City. The gun has only two bullets.
32   Male—African American stowaway who
            is a member of Mensa. An absolute
            genius. Also homeless by choice and
            antisocial. Does not like or trust people.
            Stowed away to get away from society.
            PhD in Mechanical Engineering.
44   Male—white, general practitioner M.D.
            who is, chief of staff for a major hospital
            and HIV positive.

Activity 4

1.

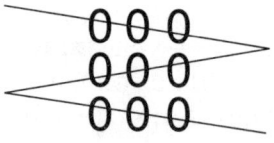

2.

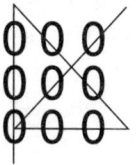

3. Circles under the eyes.
4. Two degrees below zero.
5. Neon light.
6. A backward glance.
7. Answer: Paradise.

Activity 5 Careful Listening, Better Hearing

1. White, the bear is a polar bear.
2. The match.
3. None. It was Noah's ark.
4. No. A dead person can't marry anyone.
5. No one would have known it was before Christ to call it B.C.
6. Yes, of course there is. They use the Gregorian Calendar in England.
7. A bird in the hand is worth two in the bush.

APPENDIX B: RECOMMENDED READINGS

BOOKS

Byham, W. C. *Zapp! The Lightning of Empowerment.* New York: Harmony Books, 1990.

Hausert, Thomas, and Muhammad Ali. *Muhammad Ali, His Life and Times.* New York: Simon and Schuster Publishing, 1991.

Kimbro, Dennis, and Napoleon Hill. *Think and Grow Rich.* New York: Fawcett Columbine, 1991.

Orsburn, Jack; Linda Moran; Ed Musselwhite; and John Zenger. *Self-Directed Work Teams.* Homewood, IL: Business One Irwin, 1990.

Powell, Colin with Joseph E. Persico. *My American Journey.* New York: Random House, 1995.

Shonk, James H. *Team Based Organizations.* Homewood, IL: Business One Irwin, 1992.

Wellins, Richard; William Byham; and Jeanne Wilson. *Empowered Teams.* San Francisco, CA: Jossey-Bass, 1991.

Zenger, John H; Ed Musselwhite; et al. *Leading Teams.* Homewood, IL: Business One Irwin, 1994.

AUDIO AND VIDEO RESOURCES

Ancarlo, Loren. *Implementing Self-Directed Work Teams.* Boulder, CO: CareerTrack Publications, 1993 (three-tape video series).

Archer, Ronaldo I. *Peak Performance under Peak Pressure.* Euclid, OH: Scripture Speaks Studios, 1992 (six-tape audiocassette series).

Howell, Marion. *The Manager As Coach.* Boulder, CO: CareerTrack Publications, 1993 (four-tape audio series).

INDEX

U

UAW, 56, 143
Unilateral decision making, 127-128
Unions; *see* Teams
U.S. Department of Labor, 12
U.S. Olympic Hockey Team, 16
United Steelworkers, 56

W

Wellins, Richard, 148n
Wilson, Jeanne, 148n
Workforce 2000, 12

Y

Yeager, Chuck, 68

Z

Zenger, John, 148n